Keep Your Car Running
Practically Forever

Keep Your Car Running Practically Forever

·

An Easy Guide
to Routine Care and Maintenance

Mort Schultz
and the Editors of
Consumer Reports Books

Consumer Reports Books
A Division of Consumers Union
Yonkers, New York

Library of Congress Cataloging-in-Publication Data
Schultz, Morton J.
Keep your car running practically forever : an easy guide to
routine care and maintenance / by Mort Schultz and the editors of
Consumer Reports Books.
p.   cm.
Includes index.
ISBN 0-89043-373-9. — ISBN 0-89043-372-0 (pbk.)
1. Automobiles—Maintenance and repair—Amateurs' manuals.
I. Consumer Reports Books.   II. Title.
TL152.S3915   1991
629.28′72—dc20   90-20538
                           CIP
                           Rev.

Design by GDS / Jeffrey L. Ward
Fourth printing, June 1992
Manufactured in the United States of America

Keep Your Car Running Practically Forever is a Consumer Reports Book published by Consumers Union, the nonprofit organization that publishes *Consumer Reports,* the monthly magazine of test reports, product Ratings, and buying guidance. Established in 1936, Consumers Union is chartered under the Not-for-Profit Corporation Law of the State of New York.

The purposes of Consumers Union, as stated in its charter, are to provide consumers with information and counsel on consumer goods and services, to give information on all matters relating to the expenditure of the family income, and to initiate and to cooperate with individual and group efforts seeking to create and maintain decent living standards.

Consumers Union derives its income solely from the sale of *Consumer Reports* and other publications. In addition, expenses of occasional public service efforts may be met, in part, by nonrestrictive, noncommercial contributions, grants, and fees. Consumers Union accepts no advertising or product samples and is not beholden in any way to any commercial interest. Its Ratings and reports are solely for the use of the readers of its publications. Neither the Ratings, nor the reports, nor any Consumers Union publications, including this book, may be used in advertising or for any commercial purpose. Consumers Union will take all steps open to it to prevent such uses of its materials, its name, or the name of *Consumer Reports.*

Contents

Contents

Introduction

According to current statistics, car owners are keeping their vehicles for a longer time. In 1970 the average age of a car on the road was 5.6 years; in 1975 it was 6 years; in 1980, 6.6 years; and by 1990 it had reached 7.6 years.

It is the premise of this book that there is no predetermined point at which a car becomes a candidate for the scrap heap. Furthermore, if you are able to maintain your car in optimum condition, its lifetime can be extended for many years.

You do not have to be a highly skilled mechanic to achieve this goal, nor is it essential for you to have extensive technical knowledge about automobiles. A basic understanding of how a car works will help you to prevent many common problems altogether. When problems do develop, however, you will be able to recognize the warning signs early enough to ward off costly repairs. And when the time comes to seek professional repair work, you will have the confidence to ask questions and the comfort of knowing that you made an intelligent, informed decision based on the answers your mechanic gives you.

Keep Your Car Running Practically Forever is an introduction to the basics of what makes an automobile work. Each component and system is clearly explained in nontechnical language: how an engine creates power, how fuel is delivered to the engine, how power is transmitted from the engine to the wheels, what enables you to maneuver and stop the car, and which parts contribute to a safe, comfortable ride.

The book will also serve as an invaluable guide to the principles of preventive maintenance and troubleshooting. The key to having a car that ages well is not waiting for trouble to happen; it means keeping minor problems from turning into expensive and time-consuming disasters. Being alert to what is likely to go wrong with your vehicle and knowing what to do to prevent trouble are the best ways to protect your investment in your car and to avoid the inconvenience of a car always in need of repair.

Here you will find key strategies that will help increase your car's longevity: selecting the right motor oil and gasoline, following a specific maintenance schedule for replacing those fluids and parts that most greatly affect longevity, recognizing and accurately interpreting warning signals.

Knowing what makes your vehicle work and keeping it in prime condition are essential to its good health and long life, but there is another factor: the way you drive. The last section of the book emphasizes the importance of sensible driving habits and knowing what to do in emergency situations.

Keep Your Car Running Practically Forever is an accessible resource for all car owners, whether seasoned veterans or first-time buyers. The easy-to-follow guidelines presented here will help make car ownership more economical, enjoyable, and safe.

1

The Power Team

The engine, transmission, and differential in your car, light truck, van, or utility vehicle (all of which will be called cars from here on) move the vehicle. All share equally in the task. If one doesn't work, the car won't go. It's that simple.

The engine creates power. The transmission and differential carry that power to the wheels and tires so they can rotate to move the car.

The engine, transmission, and differential are the most expensive assemblies in your car to repair or replace—so expensive, in fact, that if one of them sustains damage, the cost of repairing that damage may lead many people to dump the car and buy another.

Understanding how the power team works will help you understand and appreciate the care that the components of the team need to keep them in good working condition for as long as you own your car.

The Flow of Power

The power makers inside the engine are fistlike devices called pistons. They have arms called connecting rods that wrap around the crankshaft. The crankshaft is a long, irregularly shaped metal pole that stretches horizontally from the front of the engine to the rear. All power that moves the car, and all power that drives pumps and the generator needed for producing electricity, comes from the crankshaft.

A large wheel called the flywheel is attached to the back end of the crankshaft. As pistons and connecting rods pump up and down, they turn the crankshaft. As the crankshaft rotates, the flywheel spins. That's how an engine makes power for the car's wheels.

The operation of the crankshaft is similar to the way you create power if you pedal a bike. Think of your thighs as pistons, your legs and feet as connecting rods, the pedals and pedal arms as the crankshaft, and the chain wheel as the flywheel. The thighs and legs move up and down to turn the pedals, pedal arms, and chain wheel. That's exactly what happens inside your car's engine. Reciprocating (up-and-down) motion provided by the pistons and connecting rods is converted into rotary motion needed by the crankshaft to turn the flywheel.

An engine flywheel can turn ad infinitum, but until that rotary motion goes to the car's wheels you're not going to move the car an inch. That's where the transmission and differential come into play.

When you move the transmission shift lever into Drive or Reverse, the engine and transmission/differential (what some call the power train) couple. The energy imparted by the rotating engine flywheel is passed on to a maze of gears and shafts, which passes it along to the wheels. That's the way every car works.

A Closer Look Inside the Engine

Parallel to the crankshaft is another long pole called the camshaft. Its name is derived from the wheels, called cams, held by the shaft. The crankshaft and camshaft are connected to each other by a belt or chain. When the crankshaft turns, it turns the camshaft and cams.

Cams look like eggs: each has a narrow end and a wide end. As the camshaft revolves to put the narrow end of the cam into position, the projection pushes against a part to cause that part to lift. As the narrow end of the cam continues past the part, pressure is taken off the part, which returns to its previous position.

Cams are responsible for opening valves. Valves are devices that seal holes (or ports) in the engine. It's through these that fuel gets into cylinders and exhaust gases escape after fuel burns.

Inside each cylinder is a piston. As a cam pushes against a valve, the valve lifts and the port is uncovered.

The port through which fuel enters the cylinder is called the intake port. The valve that covers it is the intake valve. The other port is the exhaust port; the valve covering it is the exhaust valve.

Your car's engine has one or two intake valves and intake ports per cylinder. It has one or two exhaust valves and exhaust ports per cylinder. Most car engine cylinders have one of each.

The Four-Stroke Combustion Cycle

The way in which fuel gets inside the cylinder and makes power, and the expunging of the exhaust gases it creates as it burns, are basic to every engine. The process is called the four-stroke combustion cycle.

The four strokes are designated as intake, compression, power, and exhaust. Each cylinder inside an engine—whether there are four, or six, or eight, or even if there were 12—goes through the same four strokes. Here's what happens during each of them.

1. Intake stroke. On this stroke, a cam pushes the intake valve open. At the same time, another cam releases the exhaust valve to seal the exhaust port.

The piston, which has just been given a shot of energy (see Power stroke), has streamrolled down and is nearing the bottom of the cylinder. Exhaust gases that were produced during the previous combustion cycle have been purged from the cylinder. The net effect is a negative pressure inside the cylinder, that is, less pressure inside the cylinder than that existing outside the cylinder. This negative pressure allows the fuel mixture, which consists mainly of air—approximately 14.7 parts of air, in fact, to only one part of gasoline—to stream into the cylinder through the open intake port, thus filling the void.

2. Compression stroke. On this stroke, the cam releases the intake valve, which closes over the intake port. The exhaust port is still closed. The cylinder is sealed.

The piston is now swinging up, squeezing the fuel mixture tighter and tighter and putting it under extreme pressure. When it's ignited (see Power stroke), the pressurized fuel will provide a flame that will move smoothly and rapidly from one side of the cylinder to the other, thereby bringing maximum energy to bear on the piston.

3. Power stroke (also called the combustion or ignition stroke). Both the intake and exhaust ports are closed. A spark emitted by a spark plug ignites the fuel mixture when it's been compressed to about one-eighth of its original volume. The energy released by the burning fuel mixture pushes the piston and its connecting rod down with tremendous force to drive the crankshaft.

Notice we've been saying all along that the fuel mixture *burns*. It should not explode. If a malfunction occurs that causes the fuel mixture to explode, so much stress could be exerted against the piston and connecting rods that these parts could break. The damage caused would force the owner to decide whether to have the engine overhauled or replaced. A warning that the fuel mixture is exploding is a sound called ping (see chapter 5). Quiet operation is characteristic of a sound engine.

4. Exhaust stroke.   As the piston is driven down, a cam pushes the exhaust valve open. The intake valve remains closed. Exhaust gases flow out the cylinder through the exhaust port into a network of pipes that make up the exhaust system. Then the exhaust valve starts to close, the intake valve starts to open, and the whole process begins again.

The Fuel Delivery System

Obviously, an engine can't run without fuel. Most engines use gasoline. Some use diesel fuel, which is similar to kerosene and home heating oil. Engines can even be set up to run on alcohol, propane, natural gas, hydrogen, and steam. But gasoline has been and today still is the major fuel.

For gasoline to burn and impart energy, it first has to mix with air. Gasoline in the absence of air couldn't be ignited—not even with a flamethrower. To be technical about it, you couldn't ignite a flamethrower either if air wasn't present.

Bringing gasoline from the car's gas tank and air from the atmosphere and blending them before they enter the cylinders through the intake ports is the job of the fuel delivery system. There are two variations of fuel delivery systems currently used by cars. One uses a carburetor; the other has a fuel injector or fuel injectors. If you don't know what you have, find out by looking in the owner's manual that came with the car when it was new or by asking a mechanic.

What you have to do to keep this system working right depends on whether it uses a carburetor or fuel injectors. If the fuel delivery system doesn't work right, your engine is going to run badly, if it runs at all.

Carburetored fuel delivery system. An engine outfitted with a carburetor has gasoline delivered to it from the gas tank by a pump. On the way, gas flows through a filter and then through the carburetor before it enters the engine.

In practically all cars, the pump is bolted to the engine. It lies between the gas tank and filter, and has an arm that extends inside the engine. The arm comes into contact with one of the cams on the camshaft. As the cam turns, it alternately pushes the arm up and lets it drop so the gas pump (also called the fuel pump) can pump gas.

If the gas pump in your car weakens, the flow of gas to the engine will be reduced or cut off. If it is reduced, the engine will run badly; if cut off, the engine won't run at all.

When gas flows out of the pump, it enters the filter so any dirt it's carrying can be trapped. If dirt gets into the narrow passages of the carburetor, they can clog. Consequently, the engine won't get the amount of gas it needs and will run poorly.

Keep this gas filter in mind, because it can load up with dirt. A dirt-clogged filter won't allow a normal supply of gas to reach the engine. The engine will then surge and may stop as you're driving on the highway.

From the gas filter, fuel enters a bowl that's part of the carburetor. This bowl is much like the water closet of a toilet in your house. Both have a float that rises with the rising liquid. In both, the float closes a valve to turn off the flow when the liquid reaches a preset height. This prevents an overflow.

Remember the negative pressure in the engine's cylinders that we spoke about before? It enables gas and air to mix and the blend to be drawn from the carburetor into the cylinders.

Negative pressure draws gasoline from the bowl down into the narrow throat (venturi) of the carburetor. Here, it mixes with air before the blend flows into the cylinders. It's also negative pressure that causes air to rush down into the carburetor throat and mix with gasoline.

As air is scooped into the carburetor, it passes through and is cleansed by an air filter so that as little dirt as possible will be drawn into the engine with the blend. Dirt that gets inside the engine can have an abrasive effect on moving parts.

Keep this air filter in mind. If it clogs, the blend will be overly rich in gas. The terms "rich" and "lean" refer to the amount of gasoline that gets mixed with air. If a fuel mixture is too rich, there's an overabundance of gas. If a fuel mixture is too lean, there's an overabundance of air. Either causes performance problems.

The carburetor is one of the more complex devices in a car because of the job it must do. That job is to deliver a fuel mixture that is neither too rich nor too lean for operating conditions and the ambient temperature.

The elements of the carburetor that make adjustments in the fuel mixture according to operating conditions and the ambient temperature include a choke, accelerating pump, power enrichment valve, and the components of an idling circuit.

Depending on the model, there are approximately 20 to 30 parts in a carburetor. If any are damaged, wear out, or go out of adjustment, your engine is going to have a problem that results in poor performance (see chapter 8).

Fuel injection.   If your car was manufactured after 1980, chances are it's equipped with electronic fuel injection (EFI). EFI is a much more reliable and less complicated system than a carburetor.

EFI helps in the fight against air pollution, because it's able to deliver more precise amounts of gasoline and air to the engine under any given condition. A more precise blend is one that burns more completely in the cylinders, thereby producing less exhaust gases. This is why electronic fuel injection has made carburetors obsolete. In fact, almost 100 percent of the cars manufactured in 1990 possess EFI—not carburetors.

Automobile manufacturers use different names to distinguish their EFI systems. This makes it seem as if there's a multitude of different systems. Actually, there are only two: throttle body and multiport. The shortened form generally used for throttle body injection is TBI; that for multiport is MPFI or PFI.

TBI employs an assembly called a throttle body, which looks like a carburetor and is mounted on the engine where a carburetor would sit. One or two computer-controlled fuel injectors are positioned in the throat of the throttle body.

A fuel injector is an electrically operated device. When current is sent to it by a computer, the fuel injector opens and sprays gas into the throat of the throttle body.

The computer keeps the fuel injector open for the length of time needed to deliver the quantity of gas required by the engine to operate satisfactorily. When the computer turns off current, the fuel injector closes and the spray of gas ceases. The computer, in effect, is a switch that turns current on and off.

Gasoline is pumped from the gas tank to the fuel injectors by an electric pump that in most cars is inside the gas tank. On the way, the gas passes through a filter.

Air enters the throttle body through a filter that's over an air scoop. In the throttle body, it mixes with gasoline being sprayed by the fuel injectors. The blend is then drawn into the cylinders. That's TBI.

MPFI, the system used on most cars having fuel injection, is different. It has more fuel injectors, which spray gasoline directly into the engine.

The fuel injectors are screwed into the engine, just as spark plugs are, with their spraying ends aimed at the intake valves. One fuel injector serves each cylinder. Thus, a four-cylinder engine equipped with MPFI has four fuel injectors, a six-cylinder engine has six fuel injectors, and an eight-cylinder engine has eight fuel injectors.

Air enters the engine through a duct in the engine compartment. It flows through a tunnel-like device called a manifold, which contains the throttle valve. This is the valve you control with your foot on the accelerator pedal. When you press down and release the accelerator pedal, you open or close the throttle valve. This allows a greater or lesser amount of air to be delivered to the cylinders through branches of the manifold. If the engine has four cylinders, there are four branches. If it has six cylinders, there are six branches; if eight cylinders, eight branches.

Also in the manifold is a part called the air-flow meter, which is under the command of a computer. Let's say you want the car to go faster. You press the accelerator pedal to open the throttle valve wider. The angle attained by the throttle valve is monitored by a part called the throttle position sensor, which sends a signal to the computer that says, in effect, "The throttle valve has opened to such-and-such an angle. You'd better get the air-flow meter to open and supply the necessary amount of air to the engine so a properly formulated fuel mixture can be blended to meet the engine's needs."

The parts used by an MPFI system to get gasoline from the gas tank to the cylinders are the following:

• An electrically operated *gas pump,* which is most often inside the gas tank, pumps gasoline at a constant rate. The pump is outfitted with a filtering element called a sock, which traps large particles to keep them from entering and clogging the system.

• As gasoline flows out of the gas tank, it goes through another *filter,* which traps particles that are too small to be trapped by the sock.

• Cleansed gasoline flows from this second filter to the *fuel injectors.*

• *Sensors* that monitor speed, temperature, pressure, oxygen content of the exhaust, and other necessary factors determine the amount of gasoline needed by the engine.

• Sensors relay this information to a *computer.* The computer then sends the fuel injectors an electrical command to stay open for the period of time to spray the needed quantity of gasoline into the cylinders.

• A *fuel-pressure regulator* disposes of excess gasoline. Remember that the gas pump delivers gas at a consistent rate. The amount is always more than the cylinders can use. When the computer turns off current and a fuel injector closes, the excess gasoline is disposed of by the fuel-pressure regulator. It opens and allows the excess to flow into a tube called the fuel-return line. This tube extends back to the gas tank, and that's where the excess goes.

Making Fire

The job of the ignition system is to ignite the fuel in the cylinders. It does this by converting 12 volts of electric current into the approximately 50,000 volts needed by spark plugs to make sparks.

The firing ends of spark plugs are screwed into the cylinders. Practically every engine has one spark plug for each cylinder.

An ignition system is made up of two separate circuits: a primary (low-voltage) and secondary (high-voltage). The job of the primary circuit is to take the 12 volts of current supplied by the electrical system and step it up to 50,000 volts. The job of the secondary circuit is to deliver those 50,000 volts to the spark plugs in a timely and orderly manner so each cylinder gets sparked at the start of the power stroke.

The part that does the actual 12-to-50,000-volt step-up process is a coil. It works on the principle that interrupting a low-voltage current flowing through a wire wrapped around another wire that's wrapped around a magnet will induce higher voltage in that second wire.

In most cars, the 50,000 volts produced by the ignition coil flows into a distributor. The round cover over the distributor has cables attached to it extending to the spark plugs.

Voltage that flows into the distributor is picked up by a part called a rotor. As the rotor spins around, it passes current to each cable. Voltage then flows through the cables to the spark plugs.

In recent years, the distributor has been eliminated in some cars. This system is often referred to as the Distributorless Ignition System (DIS).

DIS uses a series of ignition coils under the control of a computer to make and pass high voltage directly to the spark plugs. A sensor called a crankshaft angle sensor determines which cylinder is ready for sparking. When the sensor tells the computer that such-and-such a cylinder is ready to have its fuel mixture ignited, the computer orders the applicable ignition coil to give the particular spark plug a jolt.

Juice for Use

The ignition system gets current from the electrical system. So does every electrical component in your car, from simple light bulbs to a sophisticated sound system.

The electricity-producing unit is an AC generator—AC, because the generator produces alternating current just like the current you have in your house. Also called the alternator, it is driven by a belt that attaches to a pulley turned by the crankshaft.

The generator is under the control of a voltage regulator, which maintains current put out by the generator at 12 volts, give or take a volt or two. Without regulation, the generator would deliver voltage far in excess of that needed by electrical components, including the battery. If this condition exists, those components, including the battery, will fail prematurely.

How Engines Start Themselves

The battery along with a starter make up the starting system. The battery converts the 12 volts of current it gets from the AC generator into chemical energy and stores it for future use. "Future use" arises when you turn the ignition switch to start the engine. That's when the circuit between the battery and starter is completed. The battery reconverts chemical energy back into electrical energy and sends it to the starter.

The starter is an electric motor that engages the flywheel when you turn the ignition key to start the engine. The starter spins the flywheel rapidly, which causes the pistons to pump up and down. This draws fuel mixture into the cylinders. Simultaneously, the battery provides current to the ignition system so spark plugs can make sparks to ignite the fuel. Bingo, the engine starts.

When you release the ignition key, the circuit between the battery and starter is broken. The starter stops spinning and disengages from the flywheel.

Keeping It Cool

As the engine runs, it faces potentially devastating effects from heat. The fuel inside your engine burns at approximately 4,500°F, which is more than enough to melt metal. The job of the cooling system is to get rid of enough heat so it won't ruin the engine, but to leave a sufficient amount to allow the engine to operate efficiently and provide warmth for passengers in cold weather. That warmth is delivered by the heater, which is part of the cooling system.

The cooling system circulates a cooling agent (called the coolant) through passageways inside the engine. Circulation is maintained by a pump, driven by a belt attached to a pulley on the crankshaft.

As it flows through the engine, the coolant absorbs heat and carries it to a radiator, where it's thrown off into the atmosphere. As long as the cooling system is working properly and doesn't clog or spout a leak, the temperature inside the engine will be maintained at a "comfortable" 275°F or so.

Keeping It Lubed

If it weren't for oil, friction created by engine parts rubbing against one another would quickly kill your engine. Oil lays down a protective film between parts. It also keeps carbon and dirt particles in suspension, preventing them from settling on parts and causing excessive wear.

The distribution and filtration of oil is the job of the lubrication system. The parts of this system are a pump, a filter through which oil flows to be cleansed, and an oil reservoir. The reservoir is often referred to as the crankcase.

Controlling Air Pollution

The exhaust gases produced as fuel burns have to be expelled from the engine or the engine won't run. If even a small quantity of these gases remains inside the engine, it will produce acids and sludge, which can attack and destroy engine parts. The expulsion of this waste is the job of a network of pipes, which in conjunction with a muffler, make up the exhaust system. When exhaust valves lift off the exhaust ports, gases are expelled from the cylinders into these pipes. The muffler stifles the loud roaring noise gases would otherwise make flowing through the system.

There's nothing esoteric or complicated about the exhaust system. The same, however, cannot be said of the controls that are used to reduce the devastating effect exhaust gases can have on the environment. Controlling these gases has been the greatest challenge ever faced by the automotive industry.

Not all of these gases come out the tailpipe. A lot can escape as vapors through natural openings in the engine or through openings where parts connect to the engine.

The devices developed over the years to cope with emissions, as exhaust gases and vapors are called, have been numerous and varied. The better known ones are the catalytic converter, exhaust gas recirculation system, positive crankcase ventilation system, fuel evaporation emissions control system, and air injection reaction system.

Even the computer and sensors that control the fuel injection and ignition systems exist to help in the fight against automotive emissions. In fact, if it weren't for emissions, it's doubtful whether a computer would have ever been placed in a car.

It's important to keep in mind that a malfunction by any of the emissions control systems in your car will result in greater pollution and engine performance problems (see chapter 8).

2

Transmitting and Differentiating Power

The transmission and differential are often referred to as the power train or drive train. The two work together to bring power from the engine to the wheels.

How Power Is Transmitted

In the United Kingdom transmissions are called gearboxes. This is quite descriptive, since the transmission is a box containing gears that transfer rotary motion from the engine to the differential.

Gears are attached to shafts that extend from the front of the transmission to the rear. The shaft closest to the engine is called the input shaft. Its job is to transfer the rotary motion of the crankshaft and flywheel to the other shaft, which is the output shaft. The output shaft transfers rotary motion from the transmission to the differential.

The input and output shafts are separate parts. The two are connected by various size gears on the input shaft meshing with various size gears on the output shaft.

The theory of gearing is best left to college physics texts. But without the leverage provided by transmission gears, you couldn't get your car rolling from a standstill or up a hill without placing extreme stress on the engine. This stress could contribute to the early demise of the engine.

Manual transmission. Although a manual transmission is a reliable assembly that can last for as long as the car lasts—maybe even longer—there is one part allied with it that will eventually have to be replaced. This is the clutch, which joins the crankshaft/flywheel and transmission input shaft so rotary motion can be passed from the former to the latter.

The clutch also decouples the engine from the transmission so gear rotation won't interfere as you shift the gears. Trying to shift gears with the crankshaft/flywheel turning the gears on the transmission shafts would cause gears to clash and could break off their teeth.

You operate a clutch with a foot pedal. When you let up on the pedal after moving the transmission shift lever to select a particular set of gears, you're causing a spring-loaded plate called a pressure plate to press against another plate called a clutch disc. The clutch disc, in turn, presses against the flywheel. The transmission input shaft is attached to the clutch disc, which is lined with an abrasive material that creates sufficient friction to cause the disc and flywheel to remain coupled (unless the driver causes them to disengage by depressing the clutch pedal).

The friction material on the clutch disc allows that disc to cling to the flywheel so the two spin together. Thus, the rotation of the engine crankshaft is transferred to the transmission input shaft.

When you press the clutch pedal to the floor or move the transmission shift lever into the neutral position, you're releasing the pressure plate, which takes the pressure off the clutch disc. The clutch disc, therefore, releases itself from the flywheel. Although the flywheel continues to turn as long as the engine is running so the crankshaft rotates, the clutch disc, transmission input and output shafts, and all gears slow down and come to a stop.

What is it about a clutch that will eventually cause its demise even if it's handled with the greatest of respect? That friction material on the clutch disc—that's what. Just like sandpaper that's rubbed against wood, it will eventually wear away. Also remember that springs and levers of a pressure plate are continually being flexed to bring the clutch disc and flywheel together. Eventually, stress can cause them to give out.

When you move the transmission shift lever of a manual transmission, you're sliding together a particular set of gears so power can be transmitted smoothly and efficiently from the engine to the differential through the transmission.

One set, for example, consists of the smallest size gears in the transmission. They turn at a slow speed to provide maximum torque (turning power) when it's necessary to overcome the dead weight of a car at standstill to get the car up and going. Another set consists of the largest size gears. With the car up and going, minimum torque is needed, so those gears practically equal the rate of speed at which the crankshaft is turning.

If you've worked with a variable-speed portable drill, you've utilized this same concept. Operated on its low setting, the drill chuck spins slowly to provide maximum twisting power (torque). Operated on its high setting, the drill chuck spins rapidly, providing minimum torque.

Most manual transmissions have three, four, five, or six different forward gear sets. But only two are really needed—one to get the car going forward from a standstill and one to keep it moving forward. Of course, all cars have a gear set to move it backward.

Automatic transmission. An automatic transmission doesn't have a clutch to couple the engine flywheel to the transmission input shaft. It uses a torque converter, which resembles two bowls that face one another, full of fluid.

One bowl (call it the impeller) attaches to the engine flywheel. The other bowl (call it the turbine) attaches to the transmission input shaft. When the crankshaft spins the flywheel and the flywheel spins the impeller at a high enough speed, the vortex effect created by the fluid gets the turbine and transmission input shaft moving. Gears on the input shaft that are automatically brought into contact with gears on the output shaft transfer power onto the differential.

If you doubt that fluid will create an effect like this, try a simple experiment. Place two electric fans close together so their blades face each other. Plug one fan into an electrical outlet and turn it on. When the blades of that fan start to spin, the vortex effect produced by air will cause the blades of the other fan to revolve. The power generated by the swirling fluid in a torque converter is much greater than the power generated by swirling air.

Automatic transmissions have two, three, or four gear sets to transfer power to move the car forward. All automatic transmissions also possess one gear set to move the car in reverse.

A control valve supervises the selection of the gear set needed to meet the particular driving condition. Again, fluid is the medium. The force of the fluid flowing through the control valve operates a set of levers that causes the correct set of gears to engage. The amount of pressure imparted by the fluid, and thus the particular levers that spring into action, depends on the speed at which the vehicle is moving and the load being imposed on the engine.

Making a Difference

Theoretically, the transmission could transfer power directly from the engine to the wheels. Practically, it can't. That's because your car doesn't always move in a straight line. When it goes around corners, the wheels in closest to the corner travel a shorter distance than the wheels on the other side.

The job of the differential is to make the outside wheels go faster so they keep up with the inside wheels. If this didn't happen, the tires on the outside wheels would drag along the pavement and would wear out quickly. The term *differential* is actually a shortened version of this assembly's original name—speed differential.

Depending on whether the front or rear wheels receive the power to move the car, the differential is either in the front or rear of the vehicle. If the car is a front-wheel drive model, the differential is coupled to the transmission in the front of the car to propel the front wheels. This assembly is often referred to as a transaxle. In fact, the engine sits right on top of the unit to make the three main assemblies a single package.

If the rear wheels are the ones that propel the car, the differential is in the rear between the two rear wheels. That's why a differential positioned like this is sometimes referred to as the rear end. The transmission and rear end are connected by a long shaft called the drive shaft.

Note: This description applies to most rear-wheel drive cars. However, there have been variations. For example, the Volkswagen Beetle combines the engine, transmission, and differential in one unit that is in the rear of the car, between the rear wheels. The unit propels the rear wheels the way a transaxle in the front of the car propels the front wheels.

The set of wheels not turned by the differential are freewheeling. Thus, if the front set of wheels is propelling the car, the rear wheels follow along. If the rear set of wheels is propelling the car, the front wheels roll along.

If you're curious, next time a mechanic has your car on a lift release the parking brake and try turning the wheels connected to the differential. You won't be able to unless you grab a tire with both hands and use lots of strength to overcome the resistance of the transmission and differential gears. Now, turn the other set of wheels. You'll be able to do this with one hand and a flip of the wrist.

What You Should Know About Rear-Wheel Drive

If your car has the differential between the two rear wheels, the driveshaft is connected to the transmission and differential by swiveling gadgets called universal joints—or, as mechanics call them, U-joints. There are at least two of them. One in front connects the transmission output shaft to the driveshaft, and one in the rear connects the drive-shaft to a shaft extending into the differential, which is the differential input shaft.

U-joints contain bearings. As they turn, they transfer rotary motion from one assembly to another. Thus, as the transmission output shaft turns the U-joint attached to it, that U-joint turns the driveshaft. The driveshaft then turns the U-joint in the rear, transferring all that motion to the differential input shaft.

Remember one word if you want the U-joints and differential to last a long, long time. That word is *grease*. When and how it should be applied to these parts is discussed in chapter 7.

What You Should Know About
Front-Wheel Drive

To get the differential of your front-wheel car to last practically forever, keep *two* words in mind: *grease* and *boots*. Grease protects parts. Boots protect grease.

A shaft that projects out each side of the differential transmits rotary motion to each front wheel in such a fashion as to allow the wheels to turn at the same speed when going around corners. At the differential end of each shaft is a round socket containing ball bearings. It's called a constant velocity (CV) joint. There's another CV joint at the wheel end of each shaft. There are, therefore, four CV joints in a front-wheel drive car—two conveying rotary motion from the differential to the right front wheel and two conveying rotary motion from the differential to the left front wheel.

CV joints have to be kept filled with grease to keep them revolving smoothly and intact to transfer rotary motion. Covers (boots) are placed over CV joints to keep grease where it belongs and to keep dirt away from these finely machined parts.

These boots are the Achilles heels of a front-wheel drive system and should be inspected often (see chapter 7). If a boot cracks, grease can ooze out and dirt can get inside to attack the CV joint. The repair will cost you hundreds of dollars.

3

The Safety Team

The power team is useless unless you are able to control the car. Control means stopping and maneuvering. Stopping is the job of the brakes. Maneuvering is handled by the steering system.

The third member of the safety team is the suspension system. It supports the weight of the car and keeps it in contact with the road. As long as it's in good shape, the suspension system, which consists of tires, shock-absorbing devices, and springs, also makes riding in a car comfortable for people.

The braking, steering, and suspension systems need maintenance to perform adequately for the life of the car. Knowing how they work will help you gauge what they need.

What You Should Know About Brakes

There are two kinds of brakes—disc and drum. A car can have one type or the other. Most cars have both.

There's a brake on each wheel of your car. Most cars have a disc brake on each front wheel and a drum brake on each rear wheel.

A disc brake gets its name from the disc (or rotor), resembling a discus, that attaches to the wheel and spins with it. A drum brake gets its name from the snare drum look-alike that is attached to and spins with its wheel.

In addition to the discs and drums, a braking system consists of parts that stop the discs and drums from rotating and, hence, the wheels to which they're attached. The stopping devices of a disc brake are called pads, and they're housed inside an assembly called a caliper that sits on top of the disc. One pad faces the inside surface of the disc, and one pad faces the outside surface of the disc. The caliper also contains a piston that's positioned to push the inside pad against the disc.

Pads consist of a thick layer of material that imparts friction when pads clamp the disc between them. Friction is what brings a rotating disc to a halt. In the past, the material was asbestos. Since asbestos was recognized to be carcinogenic, pads made of metal particles embedded in noncarcinogenic fibers have been in use. These are called semi-metallic pads.

Here is what happens to front-wheel disc brakes when you press down on the brake pedal:

1. Your stepping on the pedal pushes a piston against fluid contained in a reservoir called the master cylinder. This master cylinder is in the engine compartment, quite a distance away from the wheels and brakes.

2. Force exerted by the piston against fluid is telegraphed equally through lines leading to the pistons in the calipers of both brake units. *Equally* means just that—pressure on a liquid in a closed system is exerted equally throughout that system. Thus, the pressure on one piston as it pushes against the back of the inner pad is equal to the pressure on the other piston as it pushes against its pad.

3. As inner pads press against the rotating discs, the calipers slide inward so outer pads are also brought to bear against the discs. The

rotating discs are clamped between the pads and come to a stop. And with them, so do the wheels.

Rear-wheel drum brake units, although more intricate affairs, also work on the principle that force will be exerted equally to each wheel by brake fluid. The drums fit over plates that are stationary. Attached to each side of the plates are arc-shaped friction-lined parts called brake shoes. Riveted or bonded to each brake shoe is a lining of asbestos or a semimetallic material. Linings do the same job as disc brake pads: they create friction to stop drums from rotating and the wheels with them.

Positioned between the two brake shoes of each drum is a wheel cylinder. Springs connecting the wheel cylinders to the brake shoes hold linings away from the drums when the brake pedal is released.

Here is what happens inside rear-wheel drum brakes when you step on the brake pedal:

1. That same master cylinder used in the operation of front disc brakes sends equal force into the wheel cylinders of both rear drum brake units, causing arms of the wheel cylinders to extend.

2. The arms, which are connected to the brake shoes, force the brake shoes and, hence, the linings against the rotating drums. Drums are brought to a halt similar to the way you might stop yourself from swinging on a swing by scraping the heels of your shoes against the ground.

3. When you release the brake pedal, force from the fluid is taken off the wheel cylinders. The arms retract. This plus springs cause brake shoes and linings to draw away from the drums.

You can probably figure out which parts of your car's brake system are the weakest. Right—the parts that do the stopping (pads/linings) and the fluid which can, in time, become contaminated. By comparison to the discs and drums, these are inexpensive parts. Therefore, if you change pads/linings and fluid when they need changing, instead of trying to prolong their use, you can get discs and drums to last a long, long time.

Power to the Driver

Your car is probably equipped with what's commonly called a power brake. The technical term for it is brake booster.

The brake booster helps you apply the force of fluid pressure to pads and shoes, which is what you do when you press the brake pedal. In cars without an antilock braking system (see below), the booster is a canister that contains a rubber diaphragm equipped with a spring. The canister is attached to the master cylinder and is connected by hose to the engine to take advantage of negative pressure created in the engine. When you press the brake pedal, a port inside the booster closes and seals off the booster from negative pressure. This leaves a void on the engine side of the diaphragm.

Simultaneously, a port on the other side of the diaphragm opens to introduce atmospheric pressure into the canister and against the diaphragm. There's a rod attached to the diaphragm projecting into the master cylinder. On the end of that rod is a piston. The void left by cutting off negative pressure and applying atmospheric pressure to one side of the diaphragm causes the diaphragm to push inward toward the master cylinder. This helps to shove the piston against the fluid in the master cylinder, thus reducing the effort you have to exert on the pedal to activate the brakes. When you release your foot, atmospheric pressure is cut off, negative pressure is reapplied, and the diaphragm moves back away from the master cylinder, withdrawing the piston.

If something causes a part of the booster to fail, your braking system would act just like a system in a car that doesn't have a brake booster. You'd be able to apply the brakes, but it would take great effort.

What You Should Know About an Antilock Braking System

The application of electronic processors (commonly called computers) to various systems of a car has given birth to the antilock braking system (ABS).

Mechanically, a braking system with a computer doesn't differ much from a braking system without a computer. In effect, ABS is a conventional braking system served by electronic components that include a computer, sensors, and solenoid valves. There's also an electric brake booster instead of the diaphragm type described above.

There are four sensors, one at each wheel, or one sensor on the driveshaft that monitors the speed at which the wheel or driveshaft turns.

In cars having a sensor at each wheel, which is most often the case, the sensors transmit data to the computer. The computer compares the data from each wheel and, if necessary, activates a solenoid valve to allow more or less force to be applied by fluid to a particular set of brake pads or shoes.

The value of ABS comes into play when a sensor detects that the wheel it's monitoring is starting to turn at a speed that's different from the other wheels. When this happens in cars without ABS, the pad or shoe of that brake could apply more or less force to the disc or drum than is being applied at the other wheels. The result would be an unequal braking effect, which could cause the car to go into a spin and the driver to lose control.

When you press the brake pedal while driving on a slick road in a car with ABS, and one or more wheels start turning faster than the other wheels, sensors detect the difference and transmit data to the computer. In comparing data from all the sensors, the computer notes the difference and orders solenoid valves at wheels to apply fluid pressure against the piston serving that brake's pads, to bring the speed of all wheels into line. As long as all wheels are turning at the same speed, there won't be a skid.

There's no maintenance involved with ABS components. Of

course, parts can fail, but if this happens the braking system reverts to a nonelectronic status, and you're still able to stop the car.

What You Should Know About Steering

Before rack-and-pinion steering became voguish in the 1980s (actually it was first used in a car in 1905), most cars were equipped with a parallelogram steering system. The two are quite different.

Parallelogram steering gets its name from three rods that transmit your "commands" to the front wheels. The three are called the relay rod, Pitman arm, and idler arm. They attain the shape of a parallelogram when you turn the steering wheel to move the road wheels.

The longest of the three is the relay rod. It extends across the front of the car and attaches at each end to other rods called tie rods. Tie rods connect the relay rod to steering arms, which are the devices that actually move the front wheels.

Getting the relay rod going so the process begins is the job of the Pitman arm and idler arm. They're parallel to one another—the Pitman arm on the driver's side of the car; the idler arm on the passenger side of the car. When you turn the steering wheel, the Pitman arm and idler arm angle themselves to exert force on the relay rod. The relay rod moves.

The Pitman arm and idler arm are joined to the relay rod at pivot points called ball joints. Ball joints allow the swiveling effect, so steering action can be transmitted to the relay rod by the Pitman and idler arms.

The other end of the Pitman arm connects to a box that contains ball bearings and gears. This is the steering gear.

The steering column extends from inside the car, through the bulkhead separating the passenger and engine compartments, and is attached at its bottom end to the steering gear. The top of the steering column holds the steering wheel. When you turn the steering wheel, the steering column twists and activates the steering gear, which causes the Pitman arm and idler arm to swivel and move the relay rod. The steering action proceeds onward to the front wheels.

The rods, arms, and ball joints of a parallelogram system need attention to prevent abnormal wear and also to keep front tires from wearing out quickly.

Rack-and-pinion steering has been installed in most cars manufactured from 1980 onward. It doesn't require any care.

The term *rack* refers to the horizontal bar that extends across the front of the car. It's attached to the tie rods, which connect to steering arms, which attach to the front wheels. The term *pinion* refers to the gear that's on the end of the steering column. There is no "formal" steering gear as there is with a parallelogram system.

The pinion meshes with grooves in the rack. As you turn the steering wheel, the steering column turns the pinion, which moves the rack, thus conveying motion to the tie rods, steering arms, and front wheels.

Steering with Power

All power steering systems have the same parts, require the same maintenance, and present the same problem if they fail. That problem is a car that's hard to steer.

The parts of a power steering system are a pump/fluid reservoir assembly and a power steering gear or power steering rack. It works like this:

The pump is driven by a belt that extends to a pulley attached to the engine crankshaft. When the engine is running, the pump is pumping fluid from the reservoir through a line that extends to the steering gear or steering rack. The belt is the weak link and should be inspected periodically for wear and tear.

A control valve inside the steering gear or steering rack directs the force of the fluid to one side or the other, depending on how you turn the steering wheel. The fluid flows back into the reservoir through another line. In other words, fluid circulation is continuous.

The fluid won't evaporate and it isn't used up. If it disappears, there's a leak in the system. Even without fluid, though, you should still be able to steer the car.

All You Need to Know
About Your Car's Suspension System

The suspension system has two jobs to do—provide safety and comfort. These tasks fall upon the springs, shock-absorbing devices, and tires. Here's a rundown of what they do:

• *Springs* compress and rebound as they absorb shock transmitted to the car by imperfections in the road. There are two types of springs. One is a coil. The other—a leaf spring—is left over from horse and carriage days.

Your car has a spring in each corner. The two up front are probably coil springs. The two in the rear are either coil or leaf.

The springs on your car may outlive the car itself. Not that springs don't lose resiliency; sometimes they do, but not often.

• *Shock-absorbing devices* prevent motion sickness by tempering the flexing of springs. Another term for this flexing is spring oscillation.

A car that doesn't have sound shock-absorbing devices can make you feel seasick or queasy. Shock-absorbing devices also help to keep the tires in contact with the road. If there were none on your car, the bouncing of the springs would keep you airborne much of the time.

There are two kinds of shock-absorbing devices. The oldest is the conventional shock absorber, called shock absorber or just plain shock. The newest, named after the man who invented it, is called the MacPherson strut or just plain strut.

Both do the same job and work the same way. The shock or strut is a cylinder filled with fluid. It also contains a piston. The device works on the principle that fluid is noncompressible. When the piston pushes against the fluid, the piston is stopped cold. This reduces the oscillating effect of the spring.

Shock absorbers and struts don't last forever. Eventually they're damaged by stones tossed up off the road, or they spring a leak. That's when you have to replace them.

A MacPherson strut and the spring it serves are assembled in a single unit. The two have to be removed from the car and separated to replace the strut.

A shock absorber and the spring it works with are separate. Shocks can be replaced without removing the springs.

Your car may have four shocks or four MacPherson struts (one in each corner), or a strut at each front corner and a shock at each rear corner.

• *Tires* can provide safe motoring for 50,000 miles—even more. The ability to last this long considering the punishment tires receive is to the credit of the materials used in their manufacture. The rubber is still the same as it's ever been. It's used to make the tread (the only part of the tire that's in contact with the road); the sidewalls, which support the tread; and the inner liner. Credit, therefore, must go to the other materials.

The rubber parts are reinforced with belts made of steel and layers (or plies) of steel, polyester, or glass fiber. Belts keep the tread from squirming and rubbing against the road, which used to cause tread to wear away in a few thousand miles. Plies provide the strength tires need to resist impacts and punctures.

The other reinforcing parts of a tire are interwoven strands of steel wire that encircle the circumference along both edges, which are in contact with the wheel. These are called beads. They keep edges from caving in when the tire is inflated and provide an airtight seal between the tire and wheel.

If you want the tires on your car to provide the longest possible service, keep two words in mind: *air* and *alignment* (see chapter 7).

4

Preventive Maintenance

There's nothing difficult about the program we recommend for keeping your car performing satisfactorily for as long as you want to own it. The program involves these strategies:

- Periodically replace fluids and parts that can affect the car's longevity.
- Keep a watch on fluid levels between replacement intervals.
- Promptly investigate and repair the reason for an unusual noise, a glitch in performance, or any other abnormal condition.

Who Says Cars Can't Last?

In 1984, *Consumer Reports* surveyed owners of cars that were at least eight years old or that had traveled at least 100,000 miles. One star was a 1966 Studebaker Commander Six whose original engine had accumulated 548,000 miles and was still going strong. (The owner's previous car, a 1942 Studebaker Champion, didn't hold up nearly as well; it was retired after a mere 311,000 miles.) In Dacula, Georgia, a 1966 Chevrolet Chevelle V8 had gone 406,000 miles. And in Richmond, California, a 1973 Toyota Corona had accumulated nearly 231,000 miles.

Are the owners of venerable cars such as these just lucky? Or are they doing something right—something that helps stave off worn-out engines, balky transmission, whining differentials, and rusted-out metal?

To find out more about what it takes to keep a car until it becomes or nearly becomes a classic, the survey published in 1984 by *Consumer Reports* sought input from people whose cars had gone at least 100,000 miles or were at least eight years old. The response, overwhelming to say the least, brought in over 20,000 volunteers.

CR sent detailed four-page questionnaires to a selected percentage of these car owners and invited the others to write about their cars. Nearly 4,000 completed questionnaires and numerous letters were received, many of them accompanied by snapshots. Responses from those who had bought their cars used and those who work for auto makers were eliminated. In the end, we had 3,303 usable responses.

A Cross Section

Many of the respondents to the survey did some routine maintenance and repair tasks themselves. For example, 55 percent said they changed the engine oil and 53 percent said they made minor mechanical repairs.

Those who replied that they let a mechanic handle all the work also seemed to be knowledgeable about a car. Most recounted in detail what repairs had been made, and some even sent logs of the car's history.

Three-fourths of the cars covered in the survey exceeded the

100,000-mile mark; one-fourth had gone over 140,000 miles. Most of the cars (78 percent to be exact) were more than 10 years old.

Domestic cars accounted for about three-fourths of the cars represented in the survey; the rest were Japanese and European imports. Specifically, 33 percent of the cars in the survey were manufactured by General Motors. Chrysler Corporation models accounted for 20 percent; Ford vehicles, 19 percent.

Four Key Questions

The survey focused on these four questions:

1. What do you consider to be the most important actions you've taken to preserve your car's longevity?
2. How many miles do you drive between oil changes?
3. Other than oil changes, what regular services do you have done?
4. How much have you paid mechanics thus far to maintain and repair your vehicle?

The following tables summarize the answers:

Most Important Actions

Action Taken	Percentage reporting*
Regular maintenance	74
Careful driving habits	20
Fix problems immediately	13
Keep car clean and garaged	11
Use quality replacement parts	5
Find good mechanic	5
Do-it-yourself maintenance	4

*The total exceeds 100 percent because many responding to this question listed more than one action.

Miles Between Oil Changes

Interval	Percentage reporting
2,000 miles or less	17
2,100–2,900 miles	6
3,000–3,400 miles	26
3,500–4,900 miles	19
5,000 miles	15
More than 5,000 miles	16

Other Maintenance Services

Service	Once a year or more	Less than once a year	Not done	Don't know
Lubrication	83%	13%	3%	1%
Inspect radiator hoses	75	19	5	1
Inspect chassis (steering, suspension, brakes)	52	24	19	5
Rotate tires	36	32	31	1
Align wheels	35	46	18	1
Balance tires	30	55	14	1
Change antifreeze	29	58	12	1

More than one-third of the respondents reported that their cars hadn't spent a single day out of service because of mechanical problems in the year prior to the survey. And another third reported lay-ups of only one or two days.

The owners who took part in the survey were almost unanimous in their satisfaction with the mechanical condition of their cars. Only 1 percent said that their cars were nearing the end; 92 percent said their cars were in excellent or pretty good shape. The remainder fell in the so-so category.

The survey also included questions that helped to keep a check on a less than critical outlook the respondents may have had about their vehicles. For example, they were asked which of several serious mechanical problems currently affected their cars. About one owner in four admitted that the car suffered five or more problems. The most frequent problem was leaking engine oil (22 percent), followed by other fluid leaks (15 percent), and blue exhaust smoke (9 percent), which is a sign of high oil consumption.

Key Strategies You May Want to Follow

What had the owners who took part in the survey done to keep their cars in satisfactory running condition for so long? The most important strategies they followed were changing oil frequently, doing other maintenance on a regular basis, and keeping their cars garaged.

Frequent oil changes.   Without the proper amount of clean oil to lubricate the moving parts in the engine, that engine would self-destruct. Frequent oil changes help to eliminate carbon and sludge that build up inside the engine. In between changes, checking the level of oil every week assures that there is no shortfall.

There is no ideal oil change interval for every car. For your car, it may be every 7,500 miles—or every 3,000. Critically judging the conditions you impose on the engine and tailoring the oil change interval to that is the sensible approach (see chapter 5).

Most of the car owners who responded to the survey (84 percent) changed the oil filter at each oil change. This contradicts the advice given by manufacturers in owner's manuals. That advice calls for changing the oil filter at every other oil change (see chapter 5).

According to those who took part in the survey, oil consumption increased in many cars as they aged. Still in all, at the time more than 80 percent of the cars were going 1,000 miles or more before needing another quart of oil, which is excellent.

The survey results gave an indication of just how important it is to follow a realistic oil change policy and to opt on the side of caution if you're not certain what that interval should be. Responses for cars built 10 or more years prior to the survey (the cars most likely to show severe engine problems because of age) revealed, not surprisingly, that frequent oil changes were associated with a *lower* incidence of engine failure. In cars that had frequent oil changes (every 3,000 miles or less), only 15 percent of the engines had been replaced or rebuilt. On the other hand, 26 percent of the owners who followed a long oil change interval program (5,000 miles or more) had to replace or rebuild the engine.

Other maintenance procedures.   Every owner's manual and auto care book stresses the need for routine maintenance—a message that the owners in the survey had taken to heart. Three out of four reported that the most important thing they did to preserve their cars was regular preventive maintenance, such as checking fluid levels on a weekly basis, and inspecting belts and hoses at least as often as the owner's manual recommends.

Respondents were asked what maintenance they give their cars that, they believe, other car owners might not. Most stated that they were especially conscientious about lubrication of the chassis (steering and suspension) and body, and inspection of radiator hoses.

Some who replied seemed to do even more routine maintenance than necessary. About a third aligned and balanced wheels once a year or more. CR's auto test engineers, however, believe that these things don't have to be done at specified intervals. Wheels can take considerable punishment without going out of alignment. Balance is not affected unless a wheel weight is lost, which doesn't usually happen, or a tire is taken off the rim to mount a new tire. Alignment and balance should be done as suggested by on-the-road performance and the appearance of tires as they wear (see chapter 7).

The survey didn't reveal any correlation between giving the car regular service to maintain engine performance and the owner's assessment of the car's mechanical condition. One possible explanation may be that the owner of a car whose engine is performing poorly may have more of this type of service done in an effort to get better performance from the ailing engine. Another possibility is that mechanics are suggesting tune-ups rather than investigating to find the actual causes for problems.

A commonly held belief is that a car can nickel and dime you to death as it ages. You would have had a tough time convincing the car owners who responded to the survey of that. One in four reported spending only $100 or less for maintenance and repairs during the year prior to the survey. One in three reported spending $101 to $250. Only 15 percent said they spent more than $500. (Figures exclude the cost of tires.)

Remember, those are 1983–84 dollars and have little relation to costs today. Still, the comparative information showing the value of preventive maintenance is probably as true now as it was then.

Keeping the car garaged. Protecting a car from the elements, especially during the winter, seemed to have a significant effect on the car's mechanical condition. Low temperature is tough on a car. Therefore, garaging the car, even if the garage is unheated, can help alleviate problems. The survey found that engine problems occurred more often in nongaraged cars than garaged cars.

Body Language

Most of the car owners in the survey considered their cars to be respectable-looking. Slightly more than half said the car's exterior was in good to excellent condition.

Rust, which is the worst enemy, is not just a cosmetic issue. Extreme rust can weaken a car's structure and make it unsafe.

As the following summary shows, most of the cars in the survey didn't seem to be seriously affected by rust:

Amount of rust	Rust Survey Year of purchase				
	Pre-'66	'66–'72	'73–'74	'75–'77	'78 and newer
Little or none	56%	47%	40%	66%	97%
Some	33	38	41	20	3
A lot	11	15	19	14	0

Cars that were washed every other month or more often seemed to rust less than those that were washed infrequently or not at all. Cars driven in the snow belt benefited from more frequent washings than those operated in places like south Florida, Arizona, and southern California.

One-fourth of snow belt cars washed infrequently suffered a lot of rust, but only 8 percent of the frequently washed cars had severe rust problems. Obviously, it is important to quickly rinse off caustic salt spread on roads to melt snow and ice. Hosing down the underbody of a car and beneath fenders, where salt that splashes up off the road accumulates, is very important in combating rust.

The survey revealed a correlation between the number of times a car was waxed and the amount of rust that took hold. However, the results that seemed to indicate this could have been interpreted another way. A car is usually washed before it's waxed. Therefore, is it the washing rather than the waxing that prevents rust? Car owners taking part in the survey who washed their cars frequently, but seldom waxed them, reported no more rust than those who washed and waxed their cars often. Since rust usually starts on the inside of the body, engineers at *Consumer Reports* tend to be skeptical of the rust-preventive value of waxing.

Washing, waxing, or both also seem to help in the preservation of paint. Nearly all the car owners who washed and waxed their cars regularly stated that paint showed no chalking, which is a term describing the breakdown of paint into a powdery haze.

The survey also showed that garaged cars are less likely to rust than cars kept outside. Furthermore, paint chalking was reported less frequently on garaged cars.

No matter where the car is parked or how often it is washed, however, fixing dents and scrapes seems to forestall rusting. Among the cars in the survey located in snow belt states, only one in five with little or no body damage was badly rusted, while half the cars with dents and scrapes suffered a lot of rust.

Spiffing Up the Interior

Two-thirds of the respondents called the condition of their car's interior good, very good, or excellent. Nearly half said that the interior suffered from little or no wear. However, about one owner in four had put covers on at least some of the seats, presumably because the seats were worn.

According to the survey, the worst threat to a car's upholstery may be a squirming youngster holding a drippy ice cream cone. Children under 10 regularly occupied the cars of about 40 percent of the respondents. These car owners reported the greatest amount of wear to the upholstery.

Nearly half the respondents reported that they vacuumed the interior every other month or so. They also reported the least amount of wear to the interior.

Judging by the survey, cloth upholstery is slightly more durable than vinyl. Leather upholstery seems to hold up best of all; however, this may be because owners who are willing to invest in leather probably take the steps necessary to protect that investment.

Methods for protecting the interior of a car are simple enough. A set of floor mats, for example, will safeguard carpeting. Parking cars with vinyl upholstery in the shade, out of the summer sun whenever possible, will help keep vinyl from deteriorating because of heat. If water is seeping into the car, fixing the leak promptly will help keep mildew and rot from taking hold. Keeping a drop cloth in the trunk in case you change a flat or have to make some other repair and get your clothes dirty is also a good idea. Spread the cloth over the seat so you don't soil the upholstery.

5

Selecting the Right Oil and Gas
for Your Car

To keep an engine operating satisfactorily, you have to practice preventive maintenance, which means changing oil on schedule and using the correct oil and gasoline.

The All-Important
Oil Change Interval

Manufacturers claim that if criteria are interpreted correctly, the oil change intervals recommended in maintenance sections of car owners' manuals will provide engines with the maintenance needed to prevent damage while keeping the cost of this service at a minimum. The survey conducted by *Consumer Reports* (see chapter 4) suggests that engine life may be prolonged by changing oil more frequently. A closer examination of manufacturers' criteria reveals that the two points of view are in line and not at opposite poles as they seem to be at first glance.

Two oil change intervals are given by the manufacturer of your car in the maintenance section of the owner's manual. One is for *normal* service conditions; the other is for *severe* service conditions. The distinction between the two is very important.

If you have misplaced the owner's manual for your car, write the customer service department of the manufacturer for a copy, specifying that you want the maintenance schedule. Some manuals come in two parts, one dealing with the operation of the vehicle and the other with maintenance. The addresses of manufacturers are listed in reference books that are available in libraries. You can also get the address you need from a dealer selling that particular make of car.

If you drive your car practically every day of the year for at least 20 miles in an environment free of dust and industrial emissions, with at least 10 of those miles being driven on the highway at a steady rate of speed above 50 mph, in an area where the ambient temperature stays between 32°F and 90°F, you can follow the oil change interval recommendation for *normal* service conditions as given in your owner's manual.

Most of us don't drive under these conditions, however. Most of us drive under conditions characterized by manufacturers as *severe*.

Severe driving conditions are the following:

• If most trips are less than 20 miles.
• If the car is used in stop-and-go traffic so the engine idles or runs at low speed for extended periods.
• If the car is operated in an area where the ambient temperature goes below 32°F or above 90°F.
• If the car is operated in a dusty or industrialized area.
• If the car is driven consistently at an excessive rate of speed when the ambient temperature is over 90°F.
• If the car is used to tow a trailer.

If you drive your car under one or more of these *severe* conditions, most manufacturers recommend that you change engine oil every 3,000 to 3,500 miles or every three months, whichever occurs first. If you drive your car under *normal* conditions, most manufacturers claim that you can safely extend the interval to once every 6,000 to 7,500 miles or six months, whichever occurs first.

The question, of course, is where you fit in. If it's in the normal service category, but you are hesitant to adopt the longer interval, the results of an over-the-road test conducted by Honda may be of interest. It confirms there is ample latitude built into the *normal* service oil change interval recommendation of manufacturers, so following it will not cause harm to an engine even when some liberty is taken.

A number of new Honda models were driven on round trips between the Honda Training Center in Moorestown, New Jersey, and New York City—a total distance of approximately 250 miles. The course included traveling the New Jersey Turnpike (55 mph speed limit) to the city. This is one of the most industrialized and heavily traveled routes on the east coast, if not in the nation. The test also included driving the cars in New York City traffic for 10 to 20 miles, then driving back to Moorestown on the turnpike. The oil in each engine was changed every 7,500 miles, which is Honda's normal service recommendation.

When the cars had been driven 100,000 miles, they were shipped to Japan and the engines were dismantled for inspection. Not one of them showed any unusual wear or damage.

Why Change Oil at All?

The oil must be changed because of additives in the oil. These additives are used to safeguard an engine against the deleterious by-products that form as the engine is operated and with the passage of time, even though an engine might remain idle. During the normal course of operation additives dissipate, which deprives an engine of protection and may result in damage. The additives that must be replaced by changing oil are the following:

• Oxidation inhibitors. Heat causes oil to oxidize and thicken, resulting in a reduction of lubricity.

• Rust and corrosion inhibitors. As fuel combustion takes place, water and acid are produced inside the engine. They would cause rust and corrosion if it weren't for additives that keep water in suspension and neutralize acid.

• Detergent/dispersant additives. Carbon caused by fuel combustion can mix with oil to form sludge that would settle on engine parts and cause damage. These additives keep carbon, and also dirt that may get into the engine through the air intake, in suspension.

• Foam inhibitors. As oil circulates through the engine, air inside the engine can cause it to bubble. Bubbles reduce the oil's ability to lubricate.

• Viscosity index (VI) improvers. Since oil gets thicker when it is cold and thinner when it is hot, this additive is needed to change the flow characteristics of multiviscosity oil in response to changes in ambient temperature. Viscosity index improvers allow oil to continue flowing consistently so lubrication takes place despite changes in temperature.

Note: VI improvers are found only in multiviscosity oils (see below). Single viscosity oils do not contain VI improvers.

How to Select the Right Oil for Your Engine

There are three factors to consider when you buy oil: (1) the oil company that refined the product; (2) the oil's service classification; (3) the oil's viscosity rating. The first factor is easy enough to understand. You'll not have a problem if you buy oil carrying the name of a major oil company.

As for the service classification and viscosity rating of that oil, here's what you have to know:

Service classification. In 1970, the American Petroleum Institute (API), the American Society for Testing and Materials (ASTM), and the Society of Automotive Engineers (SAE) set up an engine oil service classification system. The service classification is printed on every oil container and is preceded by the phrase "For API Service"—for example, "For API Service SG." *SG* is a service classification.

The *S* portion of a service classification stands for spark ignition and applies to engines that run on gasoline. If the designation contains the letters *CC* and/or *CD*, the oil is for use with engines that run on diesel fuel. The *C* stands for compression ignition. The other *C* and *D* are service classifications. The *S* designation, usually combined with the *C* designation on containers of oil, means that the oil is suitable for use in both gasoline and diesel engines.

The letter accompanying the *S* earmarks the oil for use in certain model years of cars. Oil designated "For API Service SG" is needed by gasoline engines in most 1989 and all 1990 and newer cars. This oil contains the additives deemed necessary by engine manufacturers to provide maximum protection against wear, oxidation, and sludge buildup.

Before the appearance of SG oil, oil designated "For API Service SF" was the oil needed by gasoline engines in 1980–88 cars. If you have a car that falls into this category and you can still find SF oil, you can continue using it. Oil designated "For API Service SF" may no longer be available, however. Therefore, use oil designated "For API Service SG."

Oil designated "For API Service SE" was refined for 1972–79 gasoline engines; oil designated "For API Service SD," for 1968–71 gasoline engines; and oil designated "For API Service SC," for 1964–67 gasoline engines. Oils bearing these designations are no longer produced. If your car falls within one of these periods, use SF oil if you can find it, or SG oil.

There is a price to pay for each grade you have to go above what was originally recommended for your engine. For instance, API Service SG oil will cost you more than API Service SF, but you get more in protection.

A final note: if you find a whole string of designations on an oil container, such as "For API Service SG, SF/CC, CD," it means the oil may be used in an engine requiring any one of these designations.

Viscosity rating. Viscosity means resistance to flow. The oil you select for your engine should be compatible with the ambient temperature in your area to assure that it won't thicken and flow sluggishly in cold weather or be thinned out and flow too rapidly in hot weather. In either instance, engine parts are deprived of adequate lubrication.

The viscosity rating of oil, which is printed on the container along with the service classification, is preceded by the initials SAE—for example, SAE 5W-30, SAE 10W-40, or SAE 30. As these examples indicate, a container of oil has one of two types of viscosity numbers printed on it. They are a single viscosity number such as SAE 30, or a multiviscosity number such as SAE 5W-30, SAE 10W-30, or SAE 10W-40. The letter *W* indicates that the oil is suitable for use in winter. The terms *single weight oil* and *multiweight oil* are synonymous with *single viscosity oil* and *multiviscosity oil,* respectively.

A single-viscosity oil is restricted to a more limited temperature range than a multiviscosity oil. For example, in some engines SAE 30 oil is recommended in areas where the ambient temperature falls between 40°F and in excess of 100°F (there is no top limit). Just before winter in many parts of the country, owners of cars having these engines would have to replace SAE 30 oil with a multiviscosity oil, such as SAE 5W-30, which is able to withstand the effects of the cold weather.

This switching from one oil to another as the seasons change is the reason why most car owners prefer the latitude provided by multiviscosity oil although it is a little more expensive. SAE 10W-30 can be used in areas where the ambient temperature ranges from 0°F to above 100°F. SAE 5W-30 can be used where the ambient temperature ranges from below −20°F to 60°F.

(*Important:* The temperature ranges given here do not apply to every engine. Since engine heat, as well as ambient temperature, is a factor in selecting oil, it is important that you consult the owner's manual, which spells out which viscosity of oil is recommended for your particular engine.)

The "energy-conserving" statement that may appear on a container of oil has nothing to do with the quality of the product or the protection it provides. This statement indicates that the product contains a friction modifier to improve gas mileage. The saving is a fraction of a mile per gallon.

Caution: Before using an Energy-Conserving oil, check your owner's manual to make certain the manufacturer approves of its use in your engine for the ambient temperature that prevails where you drive.

Oil Filter Service

Should you replace the oil filter every time you change oil, or at every other oil change? Depending upon the engine, one pint to one quart of oil remains in the filter when the oil is drained.

Many mechanics and oil filter manufacturers contend that it's unwise to leave contaminated oil available to mix with new oil, and recommend changing the oil filter at every oil change.

According to auto manufacturers, the amount of contaminating agents remaining in the oil filter is infinitesimal and won't affect the fresh supply of oil as long as oil is changed at the right time. Replacing the oil filter when replacing the oil was sound policy years ago before improvements were made in oil additives as well as engine technology. It's no longer the case.

Oil and New Cars

Should you change oil more often *when you break in a new car?* Automobile manufacturers say, "No need." The high quality of modern oil plus state-of-the-art engine manufacturing techniques have made the use of special break-in oils, more frequent oil changes, and elaborate break-in procedures archaic.

Do-It-Yourself Oil Changes

Changing the oil and oil filter are relatively simple tasks that car owners can do themselves (see below). However, there is one major consideration before you begin: How will you dispose of used oil?

Environmentally conscious municipalities have established stringent requirements regarding the disposal of used oil. Service stations that agree to take used oil off your hands may charge a fee. Before changing oil yourself, therefore, find out if a service station will take used oil off your hands and, if so, how much the charge will be.

How to Change Oil
and Oil Filter

The tools and materials you will need are the following:

• new oil (Check the owner's manual for the quantity needed. Buying oil at a discount store or a supermarket is less expensive than buying from a gas station. Make sure oil fulfills the requirements for service classification and viscosity listed in your owner's manual.)

• a pouring spout or a funnel and a can opener if the receptacles holding the oil don't have screw-off tops and pour spouts

- a new oil filter and an appropriate oil-filter wrench
- rubber gloves to protect your hands
- a pan shallow enough to fit under the engine and large enough to hold at least twice the amount of oil you expect to drain
- a wrench for unscrewing the drain plug and, if needed, a drain-plug gasket (available from an auto parts department of a retail store or an auto parts store)
- one or two empty gallon jugs to collect the used oil
- rags or paper towels for cleaning up and a drop cloth or a large piece of cardboard to lie on

Before you drain the oil, run the engine for a minute or two to warm the oil so it flows freely.

In some cars, you may be able to reach the oil drain plug under the engine without crawling all the way under the car. If you're not sure where the drain plug is located, check the car owner's manual. If you must raise the car to reach the plug, use drive-on car ramps or jack stands. Never work under a car that's supported only by a car jack.

Place the pan under the engine and unscrew the drain plug with the wrench. Don't try to catch the drain plug as it comes loose. You can fish it out of the pan later. If you get oil on your skin, wash it off promptly.

If the drain plug has a small O-shaped gasket, check its condition. A hard composition gasket may be reused if it's not deformed or cracked. Some cars use a soft metal gasket that's compressed when the plug is tightened; replace that type with a new one every time.

When the oil has drained completely, wipe off the drain plug and screw it into the oil pan with its gasket, being careful to align the threads properly. Tighten firmly, but not to the point where you might damage the threads.

To change the oil filter, position the drain pan under the filter. Turn the filter counterclockwise with the filter wrench. Finish unscrewing the filter by hand.

The filter comes with a gasket—a rubber ring—around its open end. Be sure the gasket comes off with the old filter. If you can't find the gasket, it may still be stuck to the engine. Carefully pull it off and discard it.

Wipe off the engine where the filter screws on, using a clean, lint-free cloth. Before you install the new filter, smear a thin coat of oil over the filter gasket with your fingertip to improve the seal. If the filter is mounted vertically or nearly vertically, with the open end up, fill the new filter with fresh oil (for quicker lubrication of engine parts).

Overtightening the filter can distort the gasket and allow oil to leak out. Some filter manufacturers recommend only hand tightening. Others recommend tightening by hand until the gasket just makes contact and then tightening a specified fraction of a turn with a filter wrench, if necessary. Follow the instructions on the filter or in the owner's manual.

Some cars manufactured beginning in 1988 have an oil filter in the oil pan rather than screwed onto the engine. An in-the-pan filter is replaced by grasping the rim of the filter with pliers and pulling it down, then turning and pulling the filter by hand to remove it. A new filter is inserted into the oil pan and pushed up until the rim of the filter is flush with the surface of the pan.

To fill the engine with new oil, unscrew the oil filler cap and pour in the new oil. Don't add extra oil: overfilling can damage the engine. Use the plastic lid from a one-pound coffee can to seal a partially used can of oil for future use. If the container has a screw-on pour spout, simply screw on the cap.

Start the engine and watch the oil-pressure warning light or gauge. If the warning light doesn't go out or the gauge doesn't indicate pressure within a few seconds, immediately shut off the engine and consult a mechanic.

Let the engine idle for a minute or two and look for leaks around the oil filter and drain plug. If there is a leak, tighten the oil filter or drain plug another one-half turn.

Park the car on level ground, shut off the engine, wait about 10 minutes, and check the oil dipstick. If oil isn't at the Full mark, add more until it gets to that mark.

What You Should Know About Gasoline

Most service stations offer three grades of unleaded gasoline. The differences between them are based upon what many call the octane number, but which is actually a derivation of two octane numbers.

The number you see posted on gas pumps is not the octane number. It's called the antiknock index and is a measure of the gasoline's ability to resist spontaneous ignition, which causes an engine knock that most refer to as *ping*. Ping is also called spark knock, detonation, and post-ignition.

The highest grades of gasoline have an antiknock index of 90, 91, 92, or 93; the next lower grades of gasoline have an antiknock index of 88 or 89; the lowest grades of gasoline have an antiknock index of 85, 86, or 87.

The antiknock index is required by law to be posted on every gasoline pump. As mentioned above, this number is an average of two different methods used in deriving a gasoline's octane rating. These methods are the Motor Octane Rating and the Research Octane Rating. If you examine the antiknock index sticker on a gas pump, you will probably see the designation $\frac{R + M}{2}$. It means that the number designating the resistance of the gas to spontaneous ignition is the average of the gasoline's Research and Motor Octane Ratings.

Buying gasoline having a higher antiknock index than that recommended by the manufacturer in the owner's manual is usually a waste of money. However, factors may develop that might make it necessary to switch from a gasoline having a lower antiknock index to one that's higher.

As an engine gets older, it may require a gasoline containing more octane. A sign of this is the onset of pinging. A gasoline having a higher antiknock index than that recommended in the owner's manual may therefore be necessary to get rid of the ping. If this happens each time you refill your gas tank, proceed to the next grade of gas (from unleaded regular having an antiknock index of 87 to unleaded super having an antiknock index of 89, for example) to get rid of the knock.

The Role of Ping

Ping—actually, its absence—is the key factor in selecting gasoline. It is the most common term used to describe the metal-like rapping that sometimes sounds as if metal balls are bouncing around inside the engine. What you're actually hearing is the engine cylinder head vibrating. The condition is caused by an alteration in the normal combustion process that's brought on by the gasoline's inability to withstand pressure and temperature.

What's occurring is ignition of fuel in two areas of a cylinder—at the spark plug where it's supposed to ignite, and at a spot away from the spark plug. This creates two flames that move toward one another. When they collide, heat and pressure are released that put stress on pistons and connecting rods, and make the cylinder head vibrate and ring like a bell. If the condition continues, it may damage engine parts. Whether it does or it doesn't depends on the intensity of the heat and pressure.

If an insignificant amount of unburned fuel ignites spontaneously after most of the fuel has burned in a normal manner, no harm will be done. This is referred to as light spark knock.

According to manufacturers, if you notice a spark knock for a short time while accelerating or driving up hills, and it dissipates as you ease off on the accelerator, it is not a cause for concern.

Light spark knock may also be present only when you apply the brakes. If it is, your car probably has an exhaust gas recirculation (EGR) system cutoff switch that is activated when you step on the brake pedal. This produces a momentary increase in engine temperature that can cause ping. It is no cause for concern.

However, there is a problem if the ping is loud or constant, if it doesn't taper off as you let up on the accelerator pedal, or if it occurs as the engine decelerates. If any of these occurs, you should take the car to a mechanic.

The reason for an abnormal amount of heat and pressure, which can result in engine damage, is usually one of the following:

1. The engine is being run on gasoline having an antiknock index less than what the engine needs. Switch to gasoline of a higher number to determine if this relieves the condition.

2. Ignition timing is not adjusted properly.

3. The engine is operating at a temperature higher than normal.

4. The exhaust gas recirculation (EGR) system is not operating.

5. The thermostatically controlled heated-inlet air system door is stuck in the closed position, or the heat riser (manifold heat control) valve is stuck in the closed position. Your engine has one or the other, or neither.

6. Spark plugs are not the correct ones for the engine.

7. There is an air leak into the fuel system.

8. There is a restriction in the exhaust system.

9. A computerized engine control system sensor is malfunctioning.

Power and Economy

Do gasolines having higher antiknock index ratings give an engine more power and provide better fuel economy than those with lower ratings? Usually not, so you shouldn't pay extra for a fuel your engine won't benefit from.

The role of gasoline in providing economy and power depends on its calorific value, which is a measure of energy content. According to the *Bosch Automotive Handbook*, "the calorific value is virtually identical for all liquid fuels and liquefied gases."

Selecting gasoline is a preventive maintenance function. If you use a gasoline that is not right for your engine, spontaneous ignition that makes itself apparent by ping can cause engine damage.

Conversely, since most of us don't want to pay for something we don't need, using gasoline having a higher antiknock index is throwing away money if the engine will run just as well on a gasoline having a lower rating. Using gasoline with a higher antiknock index than that which allows occasional spark knock is an unnecessary expense, since occasional spark knock causes no damage.

6

Maintaining Members
of the Engine Support Team

Preventive maintenance is required by the cooling, starting, exhaust, and fuel systems for two reasons: (1) to prevent major damage to the engine or to the particular system; (2) to prevent an emergency situation for the driver.

If the cooling system doesn't get periodic preventive maintenance, the engine and the cooling system can both be damaged.

Dangerous situations may arise if the engine fails to start under emergency conditions or if deadly carbon monoxide escapes from the exhaust system and seeps into the car.

If the ignition, electrical, or emissions control systems fail, there is little chance of major damage or of danger to the car's occupants. Besides, other than installing new spark plugs and checking ignition timing at the interval specified by your owner's manual (usually every 30,000 miles), there is no preventive maintenance to perform for these systems. You should, however, pay attention to the warnings these systems issue in the form of disruptions in performance (see chapter 8).

Cooling System Preventive Maintenance

Having to pay handsomely to have a car that's overheating towed and repaired, not to mention the inconvenience and potential danger of being stuck at the side of a road, can be averted with a simple three-part cooling system preventive maintenance program. Following are step-by-step procedures.

Important: Notice that the services outlined below are called for weekly, every 12,000 miles or yearly (whichever occurs first), every 24,000 miles or two years (whichever occurs first), and every four years.

Step 1. Once a week, check the level of the cooling agent (coolant) to determine if it has fallen. Coolant doesn't evaporate or get used up like gasoline. If there has been a falloff since the previous week, there is a cooling system leak, which you should have your mechanic fix.

Most cars built since the 1970s have a coolant recovery system, which consists of a hose extending from the radiator filler neck to a plastic coolant recovery tank. The presence of this tank makes it easy to check the coolant level. All you have to do is look at the tank.

Become familiar with the markings on this tank, which are either Cold and Hot or Minimum and Maximum. The level of the coolant should be at the Cold or Minimum mark if the engine is cold, and at the Hot or Maximum mark if the engine is hot. If the markings and the level of the coolant are not clear, wipe dirt off the tank with a cloth. A coolant level that falls between the two markings is acceptable, but it should never be below the Minimum mark or above the Maximum mark.

If your car is not equipped with a coolant recovery system, the radiator filler cap has to be removed to check the level of the coolant. Do this with the engine cold to avoid being showered with hot coolant.

Place a cloth over the cap and turn counterclockwise as you press down on the cap. The top of the coolant should be approximately ½ inch below the top of the filler neck. If it is lower, have your mechanic check for a possible leak. When you reinstall the radiator pressure cap, tighten it until it locks to the neck of the radiator.

Step 2.   Every 12,000 miles or yearly, whichever occurs first:

• Inspect hoses.
• Clean debris from between the fins of the radiator.

There are four or five hoses to inspect. They are the upper and lower radiator hoses, two hoses serving the heater, and what's called a bypass hose connected between the water pump and engine.

Note: Not all engines have a bypass hose.

The reason for inspecting hoses is to uncover any that have weakened to the point where they may give way at any time, causing the engine to lose its coolant, overheat, and bring the car to a halt.

Many engines have all hoses accessible for inspection. If yours is like that and you want to do the inspection yourself, here's how:

With the engine cold and turned off, squeeze along the entire length of the upper radiator hose, the two heater hoses (they extend from the engine block to the bulkhead lying between the engine and passenger compartment), and the bypass hose. The bypass hose is a short piece (less than a foot long) extending from the top of the water pump housing to the engine. If you can't find it, ask your mechanic to show you where it is located.

If cracks appear as you squeeze a hose, if a hose feels very hard or mushy, or if you see muddy white (corrosive) deposits on the surface of the hose or around its clamps, have your mechanic determine whether the hose should be replaced.

Start the engine and let it run a few minutes. Keeping your hands away from the engine, continue the examination by looking at each hose to see if the hose bulges at any point. A bulge indicates a weak hose that should be replaced.

The lower radiator hose is checked differently. As a helper sitting behind the wheel starts the engine and presses the accelerator pedal halfway to the floor, examine this hose by shining a flashlight on it. If the hose, which has a spring inside it to keep it open, looks as if it's squeezing itself closed, ask your mechanic to check it.

Note: The lower radiator hose is a prime suspect if you ever experience overheating only when you are driving at a high rate of speed. A lower radiator hose doesn't often deteriorate and start to leak as other hoses. Instead, that spring inside the hose weakens. The spring is supposed to keep the hose from collapsing, restricting the flow of coolant to the engine. Thus, overheating at higher speeds often indicates that the spring has failed and the lower hose has to be replaced.

The other step in the 12,000-mile/one-year cooling system service is to clean the radiator. Insects and other debris scooped into the spaces between the fins of the radiator can significantly reduce the effectiveness of the radiator to transfer heat from hot coolant to the atmosphere. The radiator should be washed with a detergent and water solution, using a soft brush to loosen debris.

Caution: It is not wise to have a mechanic use a high-pressure air hose to blow debris from between fins. The strong bursts of air could bend the thin pieces of metal, causing as much of a reduction in radiator capability as the squashed bugs the mechanic is trying to dislodge.

Step 3. Every 24,000 miles or two years, whichever occurs first, drain coolant, flush the cooling system, and install fresh coolant. If you buy a used car, you should have this service done as soon as possible and then every 24,000 miles or two years, whichever occurs first.

All coolants are not the same. Therefore, it's important for you or your mechanic to select one with care.

Coolants should contain ethylene glycol and inhibitors that prevent corrosion and rust. The inhibitors don't last forever. When they dissipate, metal parts of the cooling system and engine are subject to damage. Thus, despite what the printed material says on containers of coolant you may see in a supermarket, there is no such thing as permanent antifreeze. Periodically draining and filling the cooling system with fresh coolant is the only way to replenish these inhibitors.

Ethylene glycol does not prevent freezing, so even the use of the term *antifreeze* is a misnomer. When mixed with a particular amount of water, ethylene glycol *prevents overheating*. It's true, however, that a mixture of ethylene glycol and water resists cold temperatures.

A coolant solution consisting half of ethylene glycol and half of water is suitable for most parts of the country. This 50:50 solution won't freeze unless the ambient temperature falls to 34 degrees below zero Fahrenheit.

If you require greater protection than this, a solution as concentrated as 70 percent ethylene glycol and 30 percent water can be used. This won't freeze unless the ambient temperature drops to 85 degrees below zero Fahrenheit.

Interestingly enough, a 100 percent concentration of ethylene glycol should never be used, because it turns to goo at nine degrees above zero Fahrenheit.

Important: If you live in a part of the country where the temperature doesn't fall below 32°F and you're tempted to use water as a coolant, it isn't advisable. Lacking inhibitors, water can cause parts of the cooling system and engine to rust.

If you purchase a cooling agent yourself or if your mechanic selects it for you, be sure the product is ethylene glycol and not a substitute. If the product is ethylene glycol, it will so state on the container. The right choice of coolant can have an impact on the longevity of your car's engine and cooling system.

Substitutes are available under various names. They are less expensive than ethylene glycol, but the damage they might inflict, especially if the engine and/or cooling system possess aluminum parts as those in practically all newer cars do, can cost you infinitely more money to repair.

In performing the draining, cleaning, and coolant replenishing service, your mechanic should examine the radiator filler/pressure cap, water pump, and thermostatically controlled electric fan (if that's what your car is equipped with). If these parts are damaged, they should be replaced.

Step 4. Every four years, the belt that drives the cooling fan by means of the crankshaft should be replaced. (The fan in your car is either driven by a belt or is controlled by a thermostat and is electrically operated.) In fact, to avert a possible breakdown of the power steering, air conditioner, and alternator—they are driven by a belt—all other belts should also be replaced.

Belts don't often show signs of wear or damage, such as frayed edges or cracks. Therefore, manufacturers recommend that they be replaced although they may seem to be in good condition. Tests conducted by manufacturers suggest that when belts reach the fourth year, the odds of them breaking exceed the odds that they won't break.

Starting System
Preventive Maintenance

The battery is the only part of the starting system that may require preventive maintenance. This is done to ensure starting and to make the part last as long as possible.

If the battery has removable caps, the level of the fluid (electrolyte) should be checked monthly by unscrewing the caps and looking inside the battery. The fluid level should be about ½ inch below the top of the battery in each cell (hole). If more fluid is needed, plain tap water can be added, although distilled water is preferred.

An indication of battery failure is one cell that needs refilling while the other cells don't. Replacing this battery now can help you avert the starting failure that is imminent.

Yearly, have your mechanic clean battery terminals and battery connecting points. This, too, can help prevent a starting problem. Also once a year, wash the battery with a solution of baking soda and water, and then rinse it with water from a hose. This will help prolong the life of the battery.

Batteries in most cars since the early 1970s have been of the so-called maintenance-free variety. Water can't be added to a maintenance-free battery to replenish electrolyte.

Most maintenance-free batteries have an indicator in the form of a peer-through eye, which indicates the condition of the battery. Shine a flashlight down on this eye monthly and look into it. The eye will provide one of the following indications:

1. If you see a green or blue spot, the battery is at least 75 percent charged and is in good shape.

2. If you see only black, the battery needs testing and probably recharging. Having this done as soon as possible could prevent a starting failure, especially in cold weather.

3. If the eye is pale or yellow, the battery is defective and should be replaced immediately. If the engine fails to start before you have a chance to have a new battery installed, do *not* try to jump-start using jumper cables connected to the battery of another car. Hydrogen that has built up inside the battery could be ignited by jump-starting, causing the battery to explode and showering anyone standing nearby with caustic chemicals and debris.

Exhaust System
Preventive Maintenance

Sooner or later, exhaust system parts are going to rust and fail. There is nothing you can do to prevent this. The reason for the maintenance suggested here is to detect rust-through before it happens, so you can replace the particular part at once. People are killed each year by carbon monoxide from faulty exhaust systems seeping into cars that have the windows closed.

Exhaust system parts fail most often from the inside out. Thus, rust isn't usually apparent. However, a part that is rusting makes a distinctive dull sound when tapped with a metal instrument. On the other hand, a muffler or pipe in good condition will make a ringing sound when it's tapped.

The exhaust system can be inspected when the car is raised to have the oil changed. Proceeding from the engine to the tailpipe, the mechanic should use a metal tool, such as a wrench, to tap all exhaust system parts and determine if there is a hollow, dull sound. The mechanic should also look for rust around spots where pipes enter and exit the muffler, and should make certain that clamps and hangers are secure.

If there's any indication that one exhaust system part is failing, all parts of the system should be replaced. If one part is rusting through, the others are or will be rusting through, too.

Fuel System Maintenance

Twice yearly the air filter should be removed from its housing and inspected. A dirty filter should be replaced to prevent an overrich fuel condition that can cause a performance problem and will also result in a falloff in fuel economy.

7

Maintaining
the Transmission, Differential,
Steering, Suspension, and Brakes

Periodic preventive maintenance is necessary if you want to prevent damage to systems for as long as you own your car. Maintenance is also necessary to prevent safety-related failures that could place you and the occupants of the car in danger.

Maintaining
an Automatic Transmission

Those who service vehicles for a living acknowledge that there is no such thing as a maintenance-free automatic transmission. They also agree that the service needed to keep automatic transmissions functioning properly is pretty much the same from one transmission to another.

A point of controversy, however, is how often to do this maintenance. Some say yearly; some say every 24,000 miles; some say every

50,000 miles; some even say every 100,000 miles. The time interval to adopt for your transmission should be based on how that transmission is used.

Establishing the Interval

• Check the level and condition of the transmission fluid monthly.
• Have transmission fluid changed and a new filter installed at the interval established by checking the statements of this questionnaire that apply to you:

☐ The car is used regularly to tow a trailer or haul heavy loads.
☐ Most trips average less than 10 miles.
☐ The car is used extensively in areas that experience an ambient temperature of 90°F or higher most of the time over a three-month or longer period.
☐ The car is used extensively in hilly, mountainous, or dusty environments.
☐ The car is used extensively in city stop-go traffic.

Establish the maintenance interval by adding the number of statements you've checked and comparing this number to the following:

1. If no statements are checked, have a mechanic replace fluid and filter in accordance with the maintenance schedule printed in the car owner's manual, or when the monthly fluid examination indicates that this service is necessary.

2. If one or two statements are checked, replace fluid and filter every 24,000 miles or two years, whichever comes first, or when the monthly fluid examination indicates that this service is necessary.

3. If more than two statements are checked, replace fluid and filter every 12,000 miles or annually, whichever comes first, or when the monthly fluid examination indicates that this service is necessary.

Why and How to Check Transmission Fluid

Checking the color and odor of automatic transmission fluid will tip you off if high, prolonged temperature has broken down the fluid. Keeping tainted fluid in use could lead to transmission failure. Thus, examining fluid frequently and acting upon your findings offer the best way to prevent a transmission repair that can cost you thousands of dollars.

Consult the instructions in your owner's manual concerning the procedure to follow for checking the level of transmission fluid. Criteria for reading the dipstick differ from one transmission to another. It is important that you follow these instructions, because if you don't there's a chance that the transmission will be overfilled. Exceeding the maximum fluid level can be as damaging to an automatic transmission as letting that level drop below normal.

If the fluid level has fallen below the Minimum mark on the dipstick since the last time you checked the level, suspect a leak. Automatic transmission fluid doesn't evaporate nor is it consumed. Also be aware that each transmission requires a specific type of fluid. If you have to add fluid before you can get the car to a mechanic to have the leak repaired, use a type specified in the owner's manual to avoid damage.

Whoever checks and adds fluid should have cleanliness in mind. An automatic transmission is a precision assembly that is extremely vulnerable to dirt. You should make certain the following points are observed:

• The area around the dipstick should be wiped clean before the dipstick is withdrawn from the tube.

• The cloth or paper towel used to wipe off the fluid dipstick before the dipstick is reinserted into the tube to get a reading should be clean and free of lint.

• If fluid has to be added, the container should be punctured with a clean instrument. The funnel used to put the fluid into the transmission should be pristine.

How to Detect Potential Trouble

Transmission fluid is red, pink, or green. If the fluid is some other color, it is a warning of a problem that should be rectified promptly. A minor transmission affliction as indicated by a change of fluid color can quickly turn into major damage if it isn't treated immediately.

Fluid that has turned brown or black and smells burned means the transmission has been subjected to high operating temperatures. Have fluid and filter replaced as soon as possible. Shorten the interval at which this service is done if you continue driving the car as you have been.

Fluid that has turned sickly white or pale means the assembly that cools the fluid has a leak. This assembly, called the transmission oil (fluid) cooler, is tied into the engine cooling system radiator. The leak is allowing engine coolant to mix with transmission fluid. If this is your problem, have the transmission oil cooler repaired or replaced promptly. Also, have the fluid and filter changed.

Facts for Consumers About Automatic Transmission Service

To some, the suggestion that consumers ask mechanics how they intend to service an automatic transmission may appear ludicrous. Apparently, the mechanic has to unbolt and remove the transmission oil pan, let old fluid drain, remove the old filter, install a new filter, scrape off the old transmission gasket from the lip of the pan and/or the rim of the transmission, reinstall the pan using a new gasket, and fill the transmission with fresh fluid of the correct type.

Draining fluid from an automatic transmission using this procedure, however, gets out only about 25 percent of the old fluid from many types of automatic transmissions. The remainder stays trapped inside the torque converter and will adulterate new fluid poured into the transmission.

To drain all the contaminated fluid, the mechanic may have to make the initial drain, button up the transmission, fill the unit with fresh fluid, drive the car several miles, and repeat the procedure several times until the fluid that comes out of the unit looks clean and smells fresh.

To simplify this process and reduce the cost of having it done, ask your mechanic about installing a drain plug in the transmission pan. Drain plug kits are available in auto parts stores. Even with a drain plug, the pan should be removed the first time so the bottom of the pan can be examined for particles. Subsequent drainings can be made by removing the plug.

Upon draining the fluid for the first time, the mechanic should examine fluid remaining in the bottom of the pan by shining a flashlight on it or holding it to the sunlight. This will reveal any silver or bronze particles. Although some residue is normal, silver or bronze particles indicate that one of the transmission gears is breaking down. Replacing this gear will now cost far less than repairing the extensive damage that can eventually be done by keeping the transmission in use this way.

Ways of Avoiding Transmission Failure

If applicable, there are two steps to take to avoid damaging an automatic transmission:

1. Don't spin the wheels. This applies if you get stuck in snow or mud. The inclination is to alternately shift the transmission from Drive

to Reverse, trying to extricate the car. That's okay to do, but changing gears abruptly while the wheels are spinning can be fatal to the transmission. *Gentle* is the byword. Let the wheels come to a stop before shifting. Not only will you save wear and tear on the transmission, but you'll also stand a better chance of freeing the car.

2. Consider an auxiliary transmission oil cooler if you tow a trailer. Towing puts more strain on a transmission than anything else. An auxiliary oil cooler—that is, a unit in addition to the one the car already possesses—can reduce the temperature of transmission fluid by as much as 100°F.

Important Information If You Own a Car with a Manual Transmission

The only maintenance you have to worry about with a manual transmission is clutch maintenance and to remind the mechanic to check the level of lubricant in the transmission when engine oil is being changed. If the mechanic determines that the lubricant has been contaminated, it should be changed.

If the clutch is hydraulically controlled, there will be a reservoir in the engine compartment that contains hydraulic fluid. Check the fluid level every month by peering into the reservoir, which is made of a see-through material. If the level has dropped below the Minimum mark, tell your mechanic about it. There could be a leak.

A mechanically controlled clutch requires adjustment at the 6,000-mile/six-month service.

Important: No matter what kind of clutch your car has, never rest your foot on the clutch pedal. Unconsciously depressing the pedal, even a smidgen, will cause rapid and needless wear. Also, when shifting, allow the pedal to extend itself fully between each shift.

Maintaining
a Front-Wheel-Drive System

The majority of cars now on the road are equipped with constant velocity (CV) joints (see chapter 2). They are fixtures on front-wheel-drive vehicles.

Shafts emanating from the differential are rotated by the differential to move the front wheels. Each of the two shafts of a front-wheel-drive car is equipped with two CV joints. Thus there are four CV joints in a front-wheel-drive car—two on either side of the differential and one at each front wheel.

Front-wheel-drive cars aren't the only ones equipped with CV joints. They are used on four-wheel-drive models, too, and even some newer rear-wheel-drive models use CV joints rather than universal joints (see below). If you're not sure whether your car is equipped with CV joints or universal joints, ask your mechanic.

To avoid a major repair bill, remind your mechanic to inspect the boot covering each of the four CV joints whenever the car is on a lift for an oil change or some other reason. The mechanic should turn the front wheels all the way to the left and then to the right so the area between the folds of each boot can be inspected for grease lying on the surface of the boot.

Grease warns of a defective boot. If the boot is not replaced before grease oozes out through the crack in the boot or water seeps in and contaminates grease, the CV joint will be damaged and will have to be replaced. Having to replace a CV joint because a boot that's in the process of failing isn't found costs 10 times more than replacing the defective boot.

Maintaining
a Rear-Wheel-Drive System

The components that make up the drive system of most cars with rear-wheel-drive and require preventive maintenance are the drive shaft, differential (rear end), and universal joints that connect the drive shaft between the transmission and differential (see chapter 2). The maintenance, to be done at every engine oil change, is as follows:

• The mechanic should remove the threaded plug from the differential and insert his or her little finger into the hole to feel for lubricant. If the lubricant level is so low that the mechanic can't feel it, he or she should replenish the supply with the type recommended by the manufacturer of the car on the lubrication chart that's printed in the car's shop manual.

Note: Be aware that a low lubricant level suggests a loss of lubricant because of a damaged rear-wheel-bearing oil seal or a crack in the differential case.

• The mechanic should grease those universal joints that the manufacturer has outfitted with grease fittings. There can be two or more U-joints. All, both, one, or none may have grease fittings.

• The mechanic should use a cloth dampened in solvent to wipe mud off the drive shaft. Mud caked on the drive shaft can cause the shaft to whip and create a vibration.

Maintaining Steering,
Suspension, and Brakes

Have the steering and suspension systems (and also points of the body) lubricated in accordance with the schedule outlined in your car owner's manual. Although the manufacturer may not require lubrication of steering and suspension points for thousands upon thousands of miles, this service should not be dismissed entirely. All cars need grease sometime. Your mechanic should refer to the lubrication chart issued by the car manufacturer to determine which points call for lubrication at what interval.

Services other than lubrication required by the *steering system* are as follows:

• Monthly, check the level of the fluid in the power steering pump. A falloff indicates a leak.

• At every oil change for a car that's been driven 24,000 miles and more, and then every 12,000 miles thereafter, check for a loose idler arm, Pitman arm, and tie rods of a car having a parallelogram steering system (see chapter 3).

Treating tires as part of the *suspension system,* services other than lubrication required by that system are as follows:

• Weekly and the next day after a sharp drop in ambient temperature, check tire pressure and, if necessary, inflate tires to the amount stipulated on the tire information placard mounted on the car body (usually on a door frame) or in the owner's manual. The primary reason for abnormal and rapid tire wear is underinflation. Also check the inflation pressure of the spare tire. Don't put yourself in the position of opening the trunk to replace a flat tire and discovering that the spare is also flat.

• Every 12,000 miles, have tires rotated.

Note: This is a compromise. Manufacturers call for rotating tires at different intervals ranging from once every 7,500 miles to once every 15,000 miles.

To provide the *brake system* with the maintenance it requires, do the following:

• Monthly, check the level of the brake fluid in the master cylinder. A falloff suggests a leak.

• Every 12,000 miles or yearly, have brake pads and/or brake linings inspected to determine the extent of wear and whether there is ample material left for another year of braking. If the amount of material left is questionable insofar as providing another year of service, have pads and/or linings checked again at the 6,000-mile or six-month service.

Summarizing Preventive Maintenance

As we've been emphasizing in this chapter and in chapter 5 and chapter 6, the purpose of preventive maintenance is to do what's necessary to get a car to last practically forever and, at the same time, be a safe vehicle to drive. What may seem to be a great number of services to be done at indiscriminate periods of time have been described. However this is not really the case, as the following chart shows:

A Realistic Preventive Maintenance Guide
to Help You Keep Your Car Running Practically Forever

Services	Weekly	Monthly	Every 3,000 miles/ 3 months*	Every 6,000 miles/ 6 months*	Every 12,000 miles/ 12 months*	Every 24,000 miles/ 24 months*	Every 48 months
Check engine oil level	x						
Check coolant level	x						
Check tire pressure	x						
Check and examine condition of automatic transmission fluid†		x					
Check battery electrolyte level†		x					
Check maintenance-free battery indicator†		x					

Task	Interval
Check power steering fluid level†	x
Check brake fluid level	x
Check hydraulic clutch fluid level†	x
Change engine oil	x (severe service) or x (normal service)
Check level of lubricant in a manual transmission	x (severe service) or x (normal service)
Inspect condition of CV joint boots†	x (severe service) or x (normal service)
Check level of lubricant in rear end†	x (severe service) or x (normal service)
Lubricate universal joints†	x (severe service) or x (normal service)

A Realistic Preventive Maintenance Guide
to Help You Keep Your Car Running Practically Forever (cont'd)

Services	Weekly	Monthly	Every 3,000 miles/ 3 months*	Every 6,000 miles/ 6 months*	Every 12,000 miles/ 12 months*	Every 24,000 miles/ 24 months*	Every 48 months
Clean off driveshaft†			x (severe service) or	x (normal service)			
Replace oil filter‡							
Inspect fuel system air filter (replace when necessary)				x			
Adjust mechanical clutch†				x			
Change automatic transmission fluid; replace filter†				x (severe service) or	x (normal service)		

Task			
Inspect cooling system hoses		x	x
Clean debris from radiator		x	
Clean battery cable connections		x	
Wash battery		x	
Inspect exhaust system		x	
Check brake pads/linings		x	
Drain and flush cooling system; refill with fresh coolant	x		
Replace belts	x		

*Whichever occurs first.
†If applicable.
‡Every other oil change.

Note: Lubricate steering, suspension, and body as recommended by the manufacturer in your car owner's manual. Rotate tires every 12,000 miles.

77

8

Signs of Trouble

Each system in a car sends forth distinct warnings when it develops a problem. By responding rapidly, you can usually prevent a complete breakdown and a costly repair bill.

Visual Signs of Engine Trouble

Temperature and oil pressure warning lights or gauges on the dashboard are the first signals of a problem that can cause irreparable damage to the engine if ignored. In some cars with warning lights, the temperature and oil pressure units are combined into one light designated ENGINE or SERVICE ENGINE NOW that glows if the engine begins to overheat or if there's a drop in oil pressure.

An electrical system warning light or gauge is also present in all cars to warn of a problem with the AC generator or voltage regulator (see chapter 1). Furthermore, most cars with an engine electronic control system have a warning light to caution the driver about the onset of a problem within that system. This light is designated by some manufacturers as the SERVICE ENGINE SOON light. Don't confuse this with the SERVICE ENGINE NOW light. They are two different lights.

If your car is equipped with warning lights, they will glow when you turn the ignition key but go out by the time the engine starts. If a light doesn't glow before the engine starts, consult a mechanic. There is a defect in the light circuit, which should be repaired.

If a light warning of high temperature or a drop in oil pressure appears as you're driving, pull the car off the road and seek help. Continued driving could result in severe damage to the engine.

An electrical system warning light that appears usually allows you time to drive to the nearest repair facility. Even if the engine stalls before you reach help, no damage will result.

A glowing SERVICE ENGINE SOON light means you have time to seek assistance, but it's unwise to wait too long.

If your car is equipped with temperature and oil pressure gauges, any abnormal reading—a temperature gauge that hits or almost hits the Hot mark or an oil pressure gauge that falls to zero or a little above zero—should make you pull off the road at once, turn off the engine, and have the car towed to a mechanic. Don't wait for the worst to happen.

Performance Signs of Engine Trouble

Other than through instrumentation, an engine warns that it's in trouble when it performs poorly or makes noise: if your engine starts to knock, thud, clunk, clank, or make a clicking or slapping noise, have your mechanic make an evaluation as soon as possible. Engines should not make noise except for a light spark knock (ping), heard occasionally (see chapter 5).

Other than failure of the engine to start (see chapter 11), there are nine dominant engine-caused poor performance problems that plague cars. They are defined so you can use the correct terminology and description in discussing a condition you're experiencing with a mechanic. An additional important piece of information to tell the mechanic is whether a particular driving or ambient temperature condition exists at the time the performance problem occurs, such as in slow-moving traffic, if the ambient temperature is cold or hot, if the engine is cold or hot, or if it's raining or snowing.

Poor Performance Problems Defined

1. Dieseling.   This term describes an engine that continues to run for several seconds after you turn off the ignition switch. The exhaust odor is often overpowering.

2. Difficulty starting.   After being dormant for a period of time, such as overnight, the engine has to be cranked for an abnormally long period before it finally starts. Once it does start, it may restart normally for the rest of the day.

3. Hesitation.   This is a momentary lack of engine responsiveness as you attempt to accelerate. It's as if the engine is pausing to take a breath. Hesitation can occur at any speed, but it's usually more pronounced as you attempt to get rolling again after stopping at a traffic light or stop sign, or as you accelerate to return to a previous speed after having slowed down.

4. Rough idling.   This term defines an engine that runs unevenly (hops or lopes) as it's idling.

5. Missing (misfiring). This term describes a steady pulsation or jerking of the car as you're driving at a relatively slow steady speed. It often disappears when you go above 35 mph. Putting the engine under a load, as for example going up a steep hill, often exacerbates the condition. A steady spitting sound from the exhaust is sometimes heard.

6. Poor fuel economy. A sharp drop in fuel mileage may indicate a mechanical malfunction, but it often means that the driver is using poor driving habits (see chapter 10).

7. Sluggish performance (loss of power). An engine experiencing this condition is one that delivers limited power when it's under a load, such as accelerating or climbing a hill. You get little or no response as you press the accelerator pedal down in a normal manner until the pedal reaches a certain point. Then, the car shoots ahead.

8. Stalling. This term defines an engine that quits running. If the stall is abrupt, as if you turned off the ignition switch, the cause is usually an electrical or ignition malfunction. If the engine sputters before it stalls, the cause is most often related to the fuel system.

9. Surging. This is a "want to go, want to stay" sensation. The engine alternately seems to speed up and slow down as you drive along keeping steady pressure on the accelerator pedal.

Quick-Checking
Engine Performance Problems

The engine performance problems described above have many causes. The more likely ones for each are placed at the beginning of the troubleshooting lists that follow with the least likely presented at the end. Use the appropriate list to determine if your mechanic inadvertently misses something in his or her attempt to find the cause for your problem.

You'll notice that the same malfunction is often listed for more than one problem. For example, a loss of negative pressure (vacuum) is listed as a cause of rough idling, stalling, hard starting, and other conditions.

An engine will sometimes experience more than one performance problem because of a single malfunction. More often than not, however, the signal you get depends on how a particular part fails or on the severity of the failure. For example, an automatic choke that gets stuck in the open position will cause hard starting, while an automatic choke that gets stuck in the closed position will cause rough idling and stalling. A tiny air leak into the fuel system may cause hard starting, while a major leak will cause rough idling, stalling, and/or missing.

Troubleshooting Engine Problems

1. Dieseling
- misadjusted ignition timing
- misadjusted engine idle speed
- defective or misadjusted idle solenoid of a carburetor-equipped car
- sticking choke or throttle valve linkage of a carburetor-equipped car
- buildup of carbon inside the engine (try to relieve with carbon solvent)
- stuck fuel injector of a car with electronic fuel injection (EFI)

2. Difficulty Starting
- incorrect starting procedure (check instructions in the owner's guide)

- malfunctioning automatic choke system of a carburetor-equipped car
- clogged fuel-system air filter
- fouled or damaged spark plugs
- damaged spark plug cables
- loss of negative pressure (vacuum)
- seepage of unwanted air into the fuel system
- restricted fuel filter
- misadjusted ignition timing
- damaged distributor component
- damaged fuel-pressure regulator of a car with EFI
- damaged fuel-pump check valve of a car with EFI
- stuck fuel injector of a car with EFI
- drop in fuel pump output of a carburetor-equipped car
- clogged fuel-pump filter (sock) of a car with EFI

3. Hesitation
- loss of negative pressure (vacuum)
- seepage of unwanted air into the fuel system
- sticking throttle linkage
- worn accelerator pump of a curburetor-equipped car
- inoperative thermostatic-controlled air cleaner
- fouled or worn spark plugs
- defective spark plug cables
- misadjusted ignition timing or inoperative timing advance mechanism
- malfunctioning exhaust gas recirculation (EGR) valve
- defective throttle position sensor
- clogged catalytic converter
- stuck fuel injector of a car with EFI

4. Rough idling
- loss of negative pressure (vacuum)
- seepage of unwanted air into the fuel system
- misadjusted engine idle speed setting
- faulty idle adjustment control in a car with EFI

- malfunctioning automatic choke system of a carburetor-equipped car
- sticking throttle linkage
- malfunctioning EGR valve
- inoperative thermostatic-controlled air cleaner
- stuck manifold heat control valve
- misadjusted ignition timing
- fouled or worn spark plugs
- damaged spark plug cables
- damaged positive crankcase ventilation (PCV) valve
- clogged fuel evaporation control system
- inoperative fuel-pressure regulator of a car with EFI
- damaged mass air flow system of a car with EFI
- defective throttle position sensor
- buildup of carbon inside the engine (try to relieve with carbon solvent)
- loose or damaged engine mounts
- loss of engine compression

5. Missing
- fouled or worn spark plugs
- damaged spark plug cables
- damaged distributor cap or rotor
- clogged fuel filter
- loss of negative pressure (vacuum)
- seepage of unwanted air into the fuel system
- malfunctioning idle air control of a car with EFI
- faulty fuel injector of a car with EFI
- loss of engine compression
- damage to the engine, particularly to a valve

6. Poor fuel economy
- poor driving habits (see chapter 10)
- gasoline leak
- underinflated tires
- heavy loads being carried in vehicle
- clogged fuel-system air filter

- malfunctioning automatic choke system of carburetor-equipped car
- restriction in the exhaust system or in the catalytic converter
- dragging brake
- dirty carburetor or damage to an internal part of the carburetor

7. Sluggish performance (loss of power)
- clogged fuel-system air filter
- restricted fuel filter
- misadjusted ignition timing or inoperative timing advance mechanism
- malfunctioning EGR valve
- restriction in the exhaust system or in the catalytic converter
- inoperative thermostatic-controlled air cleaner
- dirty carburetor or damage to an internal part of the carburetor
- faulty fuel-pressure regulator of a car with EFI
- clogged fuel injector of a car with EFI
- internal engine damage

8. Stalling
If the engine cuts out as abruptly as if you turned off the ignition switch, the cause most likely is one of the following:

- loose ground, or corroded or loose wire connector
- defective ignition coil or distributor pickup module
- damaged carburetor float (if the problem occurs only when turning corners)
- worn distributor shaft

If the engine sputters before it stalls, the most likely cause is one of the following:

- loss of negative pressure (vacuum)
- seepage of unwanted air into the fuel system
- misadjusted engine idle speed setting
- faulty idle adjustment control in a car with EFI

- malfunctioning automatic choke system of a carburetor-equipped car
- malfunctioning EGR valve
- inoperative thermostatic-controlled air cleaner
- damaged positive crankcase ventilation (PCV) valve
- inoperative fuel-pressure regulator of a car with EFI
- damaged mass air flow of a car with EFI
- defective throttle position sensor
- drop in fuel pump output of a carburetor-equipped car
- clogged fuel pump filter (sock) of a car with EFI

9. Surging

- restricted fuel filter
- misadjusted ignition timing or inoperative timing advance mechanism
- loss of negative pressure (vacuum)
- seepage of unwanted air into the fuel system
- fouled or worn spark plugs
- damaged spark plug cables
- inoperative thermostatic-controlled air cleaner
- malfunctioning EGR valve
- faulty vehicle speed sensor
- faulty oxygen sensor
- drop in fuel pump outlet of a carburetor-equipped car
- clogged fuel pump filter (sock) of a car with EFI

Signs of
Automatic Transmission Trouble

An automatic transmission that has a malfunction will signal distress in one of three ways: slipping, display of a shifting problem, or noise.

A symptom doesn't necessarily mean that a major malfunction has developed.

Slipping describes a noticeable delay between the time you shift an automatic transmission into gear and press down on the accelerator pedal to the time that the car actually accelerates. In other words, there's a noticeable lag in the application of power from the engine to the wheels.

There are several causes of slipping—some relatively minor, others more serious. It's recommended, therefore, that the following be done in the order of presentation:

• Make sure the fluid level is at full capacity as outlined in your owner's guide.

• Check fluid for contamination; replace fluid and filter, if necessary (see chapter 7).

• Check the shift linkage to determine if it's out of adjustment or has sustained damage.

• Find out if the transmission possesses a vacuum modulator, which is a part that controls the shifting of the transmission in relation to the degree of engine acceleration. One way to determine if this part has to be replaced is to pull the vacuum hose off the modulator, which is installed into the side of the transmission housing. If fluid drips from the hose, the diaphragm of the modulator has ruptured and the part should be replaced.

• Establish if brake bands of the particular transmission can be adjusted. If an adjustment can be made, have it done to determine whether the slipping condition is resolved. With some models, brake bands can't be adjusted manually.

If none of these services resolve the slipping problem, there is probably internal damage. The transmission will have to be removed from the car, disassembled, and overhauled.

Shifting problems occur in a number of ways, including refusal of the transmission to shift, irregular shifting, and shifting that doesn't occur smoothly but is hard enough to jolt the car. The latter is referred to as harsh or hard shifting.

As with slipping, a shifting problem may be signaling a minor condition that is resolved relatively easily and inexpensively. The fault may not even lie with the transmission. You should begin, therefore, by having engine idling speed checked to make certain it's to the specification called for by the manufacturer, the transmission fluid checked for contamination, the shift linkage examined for damage, the vacuum modulator inspected if your transmission has one, and brake bands adjusted if possible. Then, have the mechanic establish that there's no loss of engine negative pressure (vacuum), that engine mounts aren't cracked or loose, and that the universal joints of a rear-wheel-drive car aren't worn. If none of these are the reason for the shifting problem, a transmission overhaul is probably necessary.

Noise from an automatic transmission is reason for an immediate investigation. An automatic transmission should *not* make any noise—not a whir, clunk, whine, thunk.

Again, the place to begin is with the fluid and shift linkage. But once these have been discounted, chances are you're facing the expense of a transmission overhaul.

Signs of Clutch and
Manual Transmission Trouble

There will never be a doubt of a problem when a manual transmission or clutch fails. A manual transmission or clutch that has sustained damage will cause the clutch to grab (you'll shift into a gear, release the clutch, but the car won't move); the clutch to slip (engine races, but there is no corresponding increase in vehicle speed); the clutch to chatter (as you release the clutch, the car will jerk back and forth); the gears to grind (clash) as you shift; the transmission to jump out of gear; difficulty shifting into gear; difficulty shifting out of a gear; or noise from inside the transmission.

In all cases, see if the condition can be resolved by having the clutch adjusted. Other than this, there is no simple solution. In all probability, the clutch or transmission has to be overhauled. Even if the lubricant level in the transmission is low, there is a reason why it's low. That reason is a leak, which is usually expensive to repair.

Signs of
Trouble with the Differential

Noise is the only sign a differential gives to suggest that it's in trouble. However, a differential can make a sound automotive engineers describe as a commercially acceptable noise level. It's a constant, light-sounding hum that occurs between 40 and 60 mph. It's normal.

If a different kind of noise is heard or the hum is intensive, it may or may not be coming from the differential. To find out, do a road test after having the differential lubricant level checked. If the fluid level is low, this is probably the reason for noise.

Find a smooth tar or asphalt road surface. If you've not driven the car for at least 20 minutes, do so before continuing with this procedure. Then, from a standstill, begin to drive and increase speed gradually. Note the speedometer reading at which you begin to hear the noise and the speedometer reading at which you no longer hear it.

If the noise is heard while the car is accelerating, cruising, or coasting between 30 and 40 mph or between 50 and 60 mph, it is being made by the differential or tires. To establish which, drive the car on a different type of road surface. If the tone of the noise changes, tires are the source of the noise. If the tone of the noise stays the same, it's coming from the differential.

Another noise you may hear when driving at a speed of five to 10 miles an hour in a car that has the differential in the rear is a clunk. This is the sound a universal joint (U-joint) makes when it's failing. It is a sound that should cause concern.

If a U-joint fails while you're driving along, the driveshaft can drop onto the pavement. The least of your problems is being stuck in a car that can't move, because if the front U-joint is the one that fails, the driveshaft can dig into the road when it falls and catapult the car into the air. Thus, if you hear a noise from under the car when driving at a slow speed, ask a mechanic to try to rock the propeller shaft at each U-joint. If there's movement, the U-joint is failing and should be replaced.

Signs of Trouble with Your Brakes

A braking system seldom fails suddenly. Instead, it emits a warning sign for several hundred miles before the situation becomes dangerous. In any event, don't take chances. As soon as one of the following signals is received, see a mechanic at once:

1. The brake warning light on the instrument panel goes on.
2. Noise is heard as you press the brake pedal.
3. The brake pedal pulsates underfoot.
4. The brake pedal falls away under the pressure of braking and the pedal feels too soft (spongy).
5. The car pulls to one side when you apply the pedal.
6. The pedal becomes stiff, and more effort has to be exerted to bring the car to a stop.
7. The brakes don't apply until the brake pedal almost reaches the floor.
8. There is more braking force on one side of the car than on the

other. The technical term for this is brake grab, and it could send the car skidding on wet pavement.

9. The car seems to be holding back as if brakes are partially applied, as well they might be if they aren't adjusted properly. The technical term for this is brake drag.

Signs of Suspension and Steering Trouble

The suspension and steering systems signal problems by sending forth the same signs. These are a vibration that's felt in the steering wheel, floor, or seat; pulling or drifting of the car to one side although the brakes are not applied; wandering by the car over the road (lack of stability); and steering that is either too hard or too loose. The following chart summarizes the most likely causes for each symptom and what action has to be taken to correct the problem.

Problem	Causes	Corrective action
Vibration	1. Improper tire pressure	1. Inflate tires to the correct pressure.
	2. Unevenly worn tires	2. Rotate tires; replace any that are worn beyond tread indication limits.
	3. Loose wheel nuts	3. Tighten to specification with a torque wrench.
	4. Tires out of round	4. Rotate tires; if the vibration sensation is altered, check tire concentricity to find the affected tire.
	5. Damaged wheel	5. Inspect wheels; replace a defective wheel.

Problem	Causes	Corrective action
	6. Damaged or worn shock absorbers or struts	6. Replace shocks or struts.
	7. Tire/wheel assemblies out of balance	7. Balance tire/wheel assemblies.
	8. Wheel alignment out of adjustment	8. Adjust alignment to manufacturer specifications.
	9. Defective or loose wheel bearings	9. Service wheel bearings.
	10. Worn or damaged steering or suspension component	10. Replace the affected part.
Car pulls or drifts	1. Improper tire pressure	1. Inflate tires to the correct pressure.
	2. Unevenly worn tires	2. Rotate tires; replace any that are worn beyond tread indicator limits.
	3. Wheel alignment out of adjustment	3. Adjust alignment to manufacturer specifications.
	4. Damaged or worn shock absorbers or struts	4. Replace shocks or struts.
	5. Defective or loose wheel bearings	5. Service wheel bearings.
	6. Sagging front spring	6. Replace a bad spring.
	7. Worn or damaged steering or suspension component	7. Replace the affected part.
Lack of stability (wandering)	1. Improper tire pressure	1. Inflate tires to the correct pressure.
	2. Unevenly worn tires	2. Rotate tires; replace any that are worn beyond tread indicator limits.
	3. Wheel alignment out of adjustment	3. Adjust alignment to manufacturer specifications.

Problem	Causes	Corrective action
	4. Worn or damaged steering or suspension component	4. Replace the affected part.
Hard steering	1. Improper tire pressure	1. Inflate tires to the correct pressure.
	2. Power steering fluid low (leak); power steering pump failure	2. Replace the pump/reservoir assembly.
	3. Wheel alignment out of adjustment	3. Adjust alignment to manufacturer specifications.
	4. Worn or damaged steering or suspension component	4. Replace the affected part.
Loose steering	1. Worn or damaged steering component	1. Replace the affected part.
	2. Damaged or loose wheel bearings	2. Service wheel bearings.

Wheel Alignment
and Wheel Balance

The subjects of wheel alignment and wheel balance confuse many car owners. The two adjustments are *not* the same. Furthermore, the service called "front-wheel alignment," applicable in years gone by, is obsolete if your car is a 1980 or newer model. Unless it's a slip of the tongue, a mechanic who talks about front-wheel alignment is behind the times. Most cars built since 1980 require alignment of all four wheels.

Alignment is an adjustment made to the suspension system so wheels will roll straight and true. It is an essential service, because wheels that are misaligned will cause premature tire wear, disrupt steering, and even affect fuel economy. The second greatest cause of abnormal, rapid tire wear is misaligned wheels. The first cause is underinflation.

Abnormal tire wear caused by misalignment (or underinflation) can be spotted before it gets too bad by inspecting tires frequently. Look for uneven wear, such as more wear on one side of a tire than on the other, and for cupping over the face of the tire. If the signs appear and you've kept tires inflated properly, consult a mechanic before you wear out your tires.

The most common symptom of misalignment is a car that drifts or pulls to one side. Other telltale signs are looseness in the steering wheel, a steering wheel that is off-center when front wheels are straight, a sensation that the car is wandering over the road, and hard steering.

You don't have to have the wheels of a car aligned periodically. The time to consider this service is when you feel any of the unusual sensations in the steering wheel that have just been described or you spot abnormal tire wear.

Vibration felt in the steering wheel, floor, or seat of a car could also be symptomatic of misalignment, but usually the cause is one of the other reasons outlined in the chart above. One of these reasons is unbalanced wheel/tire assemblies.

You should have tires and wheels balanced when the two are disassembled. Balancing is called for, therefore, when you buy new tires or when removing conventional tires from wheels to put on snow tires, or vice versa.

9

Keeping Your Car Clean
and Bright

A car won't run better when it's clean. But it may last longer and could obtain a higher price when you sell it.

There's a right way and a wrong way to clean a car. The wrong way may damage the car and will certainly make the cleaning task more arduous.

The recommendations that follow are based on procedures used by detailers, who are professionals hired by automobile dealers as well as car owners to improve the vehicle's appearance dramatically. The tasks aren't difficult to do, and the tips and hints should help to make them less tedious. In addition, the five or six hours you spend doing this work yourself instead of hiring someone to do it for you could save you a fair amount of money.

Start on the Inside

The order in which you clean your car is important. A logical procedure assures that you won't mess up a part of the car that's already received a beauty treatment as you clean another area. Start with interior parts, as follows:

Inside the trunk, wash all metal with a solution of soap and water. Remove and wash any vinyl mat installed to protect carpeting. Then, vacuum carpeting. Sharpen the spare tire with tire dressing, which is available from an auto section of a department store or from an auto parts store.

Before leaving the trunk area, spray silicone on the weather seals around the rim of the trunk lid. This will help keep them from drying and cracking.

Inside the car, remove floor mats, put them on a clean old sheet so they don't pick up grit that can be carried back into the car, and vacuum them. Vacuum flooring, seats, side panels, and headlining. Don't neglect hard-to-reach spots such as the floor under the seats and crevices between cushions.

Is the headliner stained? Use a vinyl cleaner to treat the headliner if it's vinyl, a fabric cleaner if it's fabric. Vinyl and fabric cleaners are available in supermarkets.

Clean stains from carpeting with a foam carpet cleaner. This, too, can be purchased in a supermarket.

Next, wash hard plastic components such as the console, steering column shroud, kick panels, and rear deck below the back window (backlite) with liquid detergent and water. When plastic has dried, apply liquid furniture polish to give these components a shiny finish.

Use liquid detergent and water to wash cloth seats, including velour. Also, clean safety belts as well as fabric on door panels. Unless upholstery is stained, liquid detergent and water is all that's needed to get it clean.

Removing stains from cloth upholstery is probably the most difficult part of cleaning a car's interior. Tough stains are those made by food and beverages. Tougher stains are those made by petroleum (grease, oil, or tar) and by lipstick, ink, and crayon.

To get out food or beverage stains, use furniture upholstery cleaner. Pour some on a soft-bristle brush or sponge and apply cleaner using a circular motion. Start in the center of the stain and increase the diameter of the swirl until the brush or sponge overlaps the outer edges of the stain. Then, rub the area with a water-dampened cloth. If some stain remains, repeat the procedure.

To treat a petroleum, lipstick, crayon, or ink stain, use a spot lifter or stain remover available at hardware stores, auto parts stores, or new car dealerships. Read the label to make sure it will handle the kind of stain you're treating. Most products come in spray cans. Hold the can eight to 10 inches from the stain as you spray. Then, leave it alone for five minutes. Most spot lifters form a white residue when they've done their job of lifting the stain and are ready to be removed. Use a bristle brush or a vacuum cleaner to clean off residue.

If any of the stain remains, saturate a cloth pad with the spot lifter and press it down on the stain. Then, use a circular motion to rub the area, working the cleaner deeper and deeper into the cloth. Rinse the spot with clear water.

If your car has leather or vinyl seats, wash them with a mild liquid soap and water. After seats have dried, a coating of saddle soap, neatsfoot oil, or a commercial leather or vinyl conditioner will make them shine and keep them supple. Avoid using auto body wax on leather or vinyl. Wax may cause drying and cracking.

The one soft plastic (vinyl) part of a car that should get special attention is the dash. If not protected from the sun's rays coming through the windshield, vinyl will crack. Remove surface dirt with soapy water, let it dry, and rub vinyl dressing into the dash.

To finish cleaning a car's interior, do the following:

• Wash simulated chrome with plain water. If it doesn't come out sparkling, use a piece of extra-fine steel wool dampened with autobody liquid polish. But be careful. Use a gentle touch to avoid scratch marks.

• Apply tire dressing to brake, clutch, and accelerator pedals, and to rubber kick pads.

• Wash vinyl floor mats in a sink filled with liquid detergent and water. Rinse them with clear water and hang them up to dry.

• Spray door and window weather seals with silicone to keep them from drying out. As you do, to keep silicone off paint, hold a piece of cardboard over adjacent painted areas.

• Wash doorjambs and frames with a wet sponge.

• Clean glass inside and out with a commercial glass cleaner or ammonia and water.

The Outside

Start cleaning the outside of your car by cleaning the engine. But first let the engine run for five minutes. Then, turn it off and use a garden hose to wash the body and windshield. This is done to get the body and windshield slick so greasy dirt that may accidentally splatter as you degrease the engine won't stick.

Open the hood and remove the battery and air cleaner. If the engine has a carburetor or throttle body fuel injection system, cover the carburetor or throttle body with plastic wrap to block debris that might fall through them into the engine. Also cover the distributor, spark plug cables, electrical connectors, and other wires.

Working from the rear of the engine compartment toward the front, spray engine cleaner on the firewall, fender wells, battery tray, engine, and hood hinges. If there is a hood blanket and you can remove it, spray the underside of the hood. If not, skip the hood. Engine cleaner is available from an auto parts section of a department store or from an auto parts store.

Let the cleaner do its work for the length of time recommended in the instructions on the can. This period is at least five minutes, often more. Then, rinse everything off with water from a garden hose.

A second treatment probably won't be necessary, although a greasy-looking film may remain. That's where a wash mitt comes in handy. It can be purchased in an auto parts store.

Mix a liquid dishwashing detergent with water, slip the wash mitt over your hand like a glove, saturate the mitt in the solution, and wash down parts you treated with engine cleaner to get rid of the film. Then, hose down everything again.

To make the engine compartment really sparkle, do one or both of the following:

• Repaint the engine to its original color with a fire-resistant paint that you can buy in an auto parts store.

• Give fender wells and the firewall a high gloss by treating them with liquid furniture polish.

If your car is equipped with mag wheels, the next step is to use mag wheel cleaner, but be careful how you use it. Avoid getting the cleaner on plastic wheel emblems and paint, since it may cause discoloration.

If you have conventional wheels, there are cleaners made to treat them also, but you can do just as good a job with soapy water, rinsing them with a hose, and wiping them with rags. Use a toothbrush to reach dirt that's embedded in cavities.

You might think that the next step is to clean the "whites" of whitewall tires and apply dressing to the black parts, but hold off until later. Soap and water you'll be using to wash the body can flow onto the tires. If you clean tires now, the appearance will only be spoiled by dirty water that will flow over them.

Park the car in shade and inspect the body to find spatters of tar, road grit, and bugs. Remove these with bug and tar remover.

Bug splats often look like chipped paint, so don't ignore them. Treat anything that looks suspicious. If the cleaner removes the stuff, it's insect residue. If not, it's a chip in the paint that should be touched up.

Use a soft rag saturated with a mild liquid dishwashing agent mixed with lukewarm water to wash off dirt. Starting with the roof and working down, inundate one part of the body at a time. Then, hose it down.

After the whole body has been washed, dry it with a damp chamois. This special cloth can be purchased in an auto parts store.

Be sure to dry the tops of side molding strips, window frames, taillight housings, and anyplace else where puddles collect. If they remain, the body cleaner you'll be using next can turn to muck when it mixes with water.

If you decide that washing doesn't get the finish as bright as it should be, you have a choice of three types of polishing agents to spiff it up. The one you select depends on the degree of paint deterioration, as follows:

• Choose a liquid polish or cleaner, which is mildly abrasive, if paint doesn't show any chalkiness (whitish film).

• Choose a polishing compound, which is moderately abrasive, if the paint has a mild chalky glaze.

• Choose a rubbing compound, which is highly abrasive, on badly chalked paint. This is a last resort to restore gloss before deciding a paint job is in order.

You may even want to use two cleaning agents. For example, a liquid polish may be adequate for parts of the car not subjected to the direct rays of the sun, such as doors and the sides of fenders, while a polishing compound may have to be used on the roof, tops of fenders, hood, and trunk lid.

The important thing to keep in mind is to use the least abrasive agent possible on each individual body panel. The more abrasive a polishing agent, the more it will remove. Brightness is restored to a car's body by rubbing off "dead" paint so the glossy paint beneath it is revealed. By rubbing off paint that hasn't deteriorated, you shorten the time until the car needs repainting.

You can polish a car by hand or by using a buffer/polisher, also called an orbiter. Do not use a power drill equipped with a buffing pad. The tendency is to tip the drill and press down so the edge of the pad is concentrated heavily against the paint. This can cut through the paint and damage the primer.

An orbiter, on the other hand, has a large, thick rotary buffing pad. The tool is designed to make you apply the entire flat surface of this pad against the car with relatively light pressure. You can rent an orbiter from a rental store that carries automotive tools.

After you've polished the body, look for residue caught in cracks around moldings, lamp housings, and gutters. Remove this with a soft-bristle toothbrush.

Now apply wax to the body. Only one application is necessary. Two or more won't provide any greater protection.

Contrary to popular belief, wax doesn't give paint a gloss. The polishing agent does. The job of wax is to protect the finish.

Between cleanings, you can tell if the finish should have another coating of wax applied to it by watching how drops of water form on the body when it's raining. Water that forms nearly spherical beads means that wax is sufficient. When water forms quarter-size puddles, it's time to apply another coat.

The final task is to give exterior parts their own dressup treatment. Use a vinyl cleaner on vinyl tops, vinyl moldings, and urethane or polypropylene bumpers. After cleaning a black plastic bumper, apply a coat of black shoe polish wax to make the bumper shine.

Clean simulated chrome with a household cleaner. If parts don't come out sparkling, they may need a stronger treatment, so try extra-fine steel wool that's saturated with a liquid body polish. But apply it gently to avoid scratches.

Finally, sharpen up tires with whitewall cleaner and tire dressing.

10

The Benefits
of Sensible Driving

Driving your car sensibly pays dividends in three ways. First, it prolongs the life of mechanical components and helps to keep the car trouble-free. Second, it conserves gasoline, saving you money. Third, it's safer.

The Break-in Period

Driving a brand-new car with a mind to keeping it trouble-free begins the day you take it from the dealership. Although it is not necessary, as it once was, to gradually increase the speed at which you drive over a specific number of miles and to drain and flush lubricants early in the car's life, there are these procedures to follow to minimize wear and tear on mechanical systems:

1. Don't drive for long stretches at a constant speed. For the first 1,000 miles, vary speed every 10 miles or so as driving conditions

permit. Accelerate moderately above the speed at which you've been traveling for a second or two; then, take your foot off the accelerator pedal to let speed drop for another couple of seconds before resuming your original speed.

2. Don't avoid driving at highway speeds. Higher-speed driving is necessary for piston rings to seat themselves properly against the walls of the cylinders; otherwise, the engine will consume an excessive amount of oil.

3. Avoid tire-screeching fast starts to prevent transmission and clutch damage.

4. Try to avoid panic stops. New linings or disc-brake pads never exactly match the contours of brake drums or rotors. Until high spots wear down so the full surface of linings or pads come into contact with drums or discs, panic-stop braking can cause linings or pads to overheat and form a glaze over their surfaces. The glaze will reduce the efficiency of brakes.

Facts About
Cold Engine Operation

Over the years, misinformation has been passed along about how to treat an engine that's started first thing in the morning, especially on cold days. Here are the facts:

Don't race a cold engine and don't accelerate hard until the engine is warm.

Don't let an engine you've just started idle for longer than 30 seconds. More wear and tear is placed on a cold engine that is kept idling until the cooling system gets hot enough to expel warm air from the heater rather than starting the engine and driving off at a moderate rate of speed.

Protecting Other Systems

Here are other techniques to use that will help prevent unnecessary wear and tear on major components as you drive your car:

• As you shift a manual transmission into a higher gear, let engine speed drop slightly so the clutch can engage without a jerk. When you shift to a lower gear, rev the engine a bit so the clutch engages smoothly.

• Don't ram the shift lever into gear. Shift deliberately, pausing for an instant as you move the lever through the neutral position. This will prevent unnecessary strain on synchronizers in the transmission.

• Whether you have a manual or automatic transmission, avoid shifting into a forward gear while the car is rolling backward. Avoid shifting into Reverse while the car is rolling forward.

• When you stop in traffic on a hill, hold the car in place with the brakes. Don't race the engine to keep from rolling back, which places undue stress on the engine. Partially engaging a clutch as you race the engine puts unnecessary wear on the clutch.

• Never rest your foot on the clutch pedal while you're driving. Riding the clutch will cause the clutch to wear prematurely.

• When you have to stop for more than a few seconds with the engine idling, such as at a drawbridge or railroad crossing, shift into Neutral and release the clutch pedal or turn off the engine. Sitting with the pedal depressed increases wear on the throw-out bearing, which is that part of the mechanism that disengages the clutch when you step on the pedal.

• Don't turn the steering wheel while the car is motionless. You'll put strain on front-end components.

• Try to steer around or straddle potholes. If you can't avoid one, try to roll over the bump at an angle without applying the brake. This technique helps prevent steering and suspension damage and should be followed when crossing other bumpy areas, such as railroad tracks.

Driving to Achieve Maximum MPG

During the oil crisis of 1979, tests conducted by the U.S. Department of Energy (DOE) and Atlantic Richfield Company (ARCO) proved that drivers could improve gas mileage by 20 to 30 percent using the driving techniques described here. These techniques are as valid today as they were then and can translate into a considerable saving.

Let's assume a weekly fill-up of your car's gas tank requires 15 gallons. That's 780 gallons a year. A saving of 20 to 30 percent means a reduction of 156 to 234 gallons per year that you have to buy. Using $1.25 as the representative price for a gallon of gas, you conceivably could save $195 to $292 per year by using these proven methods:

1. Drive at the speed limit. When that limit was 55 mph, those who abided by it realized a 15 to 18 percent saving in fuel costs compared to those who drove at 60 mph and more.

2. Don't tailgate and don't cut in and out of traffic. Using brakes constantly to slow down and then accelerating when spotting an opening wastes gas and also causes unnecessary brake wear.

3. When approaching a red traffic light, slow down by taking your foot off the accelerator pedal. Try to reach the light when it's green so you don't have to stop.

4. Apply brakes with your right foot. People who use their left foot often unconsciously keep light pressure on the accelerator pedal with their right foot, allowing the engine to burn gas needlessly.

5. Keep windows closed when driving on the highway. In warm weather, less gas is used when the air conditioner is operating than by having the car buck the wind resistance it would encounter with the windows open.

6. In cold weather, keep the heater blower on the lowest setting.

7. Drive slower when the car is bucking a head wind. Wind resistance is a key factor in reducing gas mileage at speeds over 40 mph.

8. If you're waiting in a parked car for someone, don't let the engine idle for more than a minute. You save gas by shutting the engine off and restarting it when you're ready to go.

9. Avoid unnecessary steering wheel movement. Sideward movement of the tires causes drag, which increases fuel consumption.

10. Accelerate to cruising speed as rapidly but as smoothly as possible. Avoid jackrabbit starts.

11. Accelerate slowly on sand, gravel, and snowy, icy, or rain-slick roads to keep tires from spinning.

12. Going uphill, gently press the accelerator pedal and maintain just enough momentum to carry you over the top. Once over the crest, ease off on the accelerator pedal and let gravity help you down the other side.

13. Use a speed (cruise) control system whenever possible.

14. Keep tires inflated to the pressure recommended by the manufacturer.

15. Be sure the fuel-system air filter is clean.

16. Keep drive belts tightened to the manufacturer's specification.

17. Change engine oil when you should (see chapter 5).

11

Coping with Emergencies

The best way to avoid an emergency on the road is to take steps to prevent that emergency from happening. Therefore, once every other week, check parts that are most likely to fail and leave you stranded. Parts that can compromise safety should also be inspected.

Biweekly Checkpoints

1. Tires
• Set inflation pressure of all tires, including the spare, to manufacturer's recommendation.

• Look for bulges in the tread and sidewalls of each tire and for cuts in the sidewalls. This includes the spare. Have a mechanic judge whether the bulge or cut constitutes a hazard.

• Make sure treads of tires, including the spare, aren't worn to the danger level.

2. Brakes

• Start the engine and step on the brake pedal. It should feel firm.

• Does the brake pedal fall below the level of the accelerator pedal? This may be a sign that pads or linings are worn.

• While driving at 10 to 15 mph, apply normal pressure to the brake pedal to bring the car to a stop. If brakes grab or the car veers to one side, brakes need repair.

3. Hoses and Belts

• Squeeze cooling system hoses. They should feel firm and not show any cracks.

• Examine drive belts for cracks and cuts.

4. Steering and suspension

• While driving, determine if the car wanders from side to side. If so and tires are properly inflated, have a mechanic check for worn shock absorbers or struts.

5. Windshield wipers/washers

• Do wiper blades streak the glass? Clean them and the glass with ammonia and water. If streaking recurs, the blades should be replaced.

• If a wiper arm is bent, replace it.

• Make sure the washer reservoir is filled. Test washers. If they don't work, have a mechanic inspect the filter and hose in the washer reservoir.

6. Lights and horn

• Do high and low beams work?

• Do parking lights, side-marker lights, turn signals, emergency flashers, taillights, braking (stop) lights, and the license plate light glow?

• Does the horn sound?

Tool Kit
for a Road Emergency

You can't be prepared for every possible road emergency, but carrying the following equipment in the car can help you handle some of the most frequent problems you're liable to encounter:

Road emergency signals. Triangular reflectors and flares (for use in fog) will help other motorists avoid running into your car as you make repairs or wait for help.

Jack. Familiarize yourself with the jacking points for your car. This information is usually on a decal in the trunk and can also be found in your owner's guide.

Wheel chock. A tapered wooden wedge that's about three inches on the thick end will help keep a car stable as you jack it. Place the chock behind the rear wheel that's diagonal to a front wheel that is being raised or in front of the front wheel that's diagonal to a rear wheel that is being raised.

Jack support. A piece of ¾-inch plywood that's about a foot square on which to put the jack will keep it from sinking into soft, muddy ground.

Lug wrench. This is a piece of equipment that comes with a new car.

Tire pump. Pumping up a tire that has a slow leak and driving to a service station is less strenuous and hazardous than changing the tire at the side of a heavily traveled roadway.

Trouble light or flashlight. A trouble light plugs into the cigarette lighter. A flashlight requires frequent checks to make sure the batteries are strong.

Fire extinguisher. Keep a UL-approved fire extinguisher in the passenger compartment so it's within easy reach. Check the indicator dial regularly to make sure pressure is adequate. Fire extinguishers should not be stored where temperatures could exceed 120°F.

Assorted hand tools. Various size open-end wrenches, conventional and Phillips-head screwdrivers, pliers, penknife, and hammer may come in handy.

Metal fuel container and funnel. Carry an empty metal fuel container, since many service stations won't lend you one if you run out of gas and have to carry a gallon or two back to your car. Don't carry fuel in the car. It's too dangerous.

Siphon. If you have a siphon, you may be able to buy a gallon or two of gas from a passing motorist when there is no service station available. Buy a siphon that has a squeeze tube. Never draw gas from a gas tank using your mouth and a conventional hose. Accidentally swallowing gasoline can be fatal.

Duct or electrical tape. This is useful for temporarily sealing a leaking cooling system hose.

Wire coat hanger. This is useful for temporarily supporting an exhaust system pipe that breaks free.

Fuses. Carry a spare of each type that your car requires. Consult with a mechanic to determine which types of fuses you need.

First-aid kit. Include bandages and antiseptic.

Pad and pencil. If involved in an accident, you'll need these to record the details.

Coins. Tape coins under the dashboard for use in an emergency in a pay telephone.

Booster cables. Booster cables can often get the engine started if the battery goes dead (see below).

Getting Towed

If you get stuck by the roadside, you may have to be towed. Unless the tow truck operator uses the correct towing procedure for your particular vehicle, extensive structural and cosmetic damage can result. Your best defense is knowing what the operator should be doing.

Anticipating that a day will come when you'll have to be towed, find out the towing procedure recommended for your vehicle by the manufacturer. Ask the dealer from whom you bought the car or check with your mechanic. You can also buy a towing manual published annually by the American Automobile Association, 1000 AAA Drive, Heathrow, FL 32746. The manual provides instruction and diagrams for how to tow every make and model of car manufactured in a particular year. Be sure to mention the year and model of your car. Don't use data that applies to your model car built in any year except the year you own. Towing instructions may have changed from one year to the next for the same model. Keep a copy of the towing instructions for your car in the glove compartment.

If you're a member of a motor club, don't be complacent. You're not immune from shoddy towing methods. Many motor clubs protect members by holding towing companies they recommend accountable for damage they cause. But this doesn't compensate you for the time, trouble, and aggravation of having an operator make a mistake that damages your vehicle.

The first step in having your car towed is to decide which towing service to call. If you are within reasonable distance of a repair facility you usually patronize, find out if they can do the towing.

If you're a member of a motor club and use a towing company the club recommends, check the instructions for contacting the company provided by the club. That material should be kept in your car's glove compartment.

If you aren't a member of a motor club and have to find a towing company on your own, look under "Towing" in the classified pages of the telephone book for a company that advertises its affiliation with a motor club, which indicates a degree of competency. An alternative is to call the police and ask the dispatcher to recommend a reliable operator.

When you have the towing company on the phone, make sure you relate or elicit the following information:

- The make, model, and year of the vehicle.
- If the transmission or differential is inoperable.
- If the car has special equipment such as fog lights, air dam, extra-wide tires, or spoilers.
- If a trailer is hitched to the car.
- If you drive a pickup truck, whether it has a camper body, is fully loaded, or has a trailer hitched to it.
- If you have passengers with you, whether the towing company can make transportation arrangements for them. Passengers can't ride in the car as it's being towed, since laws prohibit this dangerous practice.
- Where the vehicle is located and where you want it towed.
- Price and method of payment (some firms take only cash).
- The kind of vehicle the company intends to provide. It will either be a sling, wheel-lift, or flatbed tow truck. You need this information to compare with the information you have about how your car should be towed to make sure the correct vehicle will be dispatched.

Sling equipment incorporates a pair of wide flexible straps on a tow bar, which wrap around and cradle the raised end of the car.

Wheel-lift equipment positions a platform under front or rear tires. Platforms grasp the tires and a hydraulic arm lifts the car.

A hydraulic pulley of a flatbed wrecker pulls the car onto the flatbed of this truck. The car is tied down so it's secure while it's transported.

The tow truck that's dispatched should also carry auxiliary equipment necessary for towing the car, such as a 4 × 4-inch crossbeam, spacer blocks, or a wheel dolly. Damage to the car's bumpers, radiator, suspension parts, frame, or transmission may result if a stipulated piece of equipment is not used.

Before the tow truck operator takes the car in tow, conduct a walk-around inspection with him or her. Make two lists of existing damage. Give one to the operator and retain the other. Have the operator sign your list. You sign the operator's list.

A car should always be towed with its drive wheels off the ground. These are the rear wheels of a car with the differential in the rear; the front wheels of a car with the differential in the front. If the end of the car without the differential can't be raised, the drive wheels must be placed on a wheel dolly so the dolly, not the drive wheels, rolls on the pavement to prevent damaging the differential. An alternative is to disconnect the driveshaft of a car with the differential in the rear.

If your vehicle is equipped with four-wheel drive, disengage the power takeoff to free the front wheels. Then, the rear of the vehicle can be raised.

Before the tow begins, the transmission should be placed in Neutral and the parking brake should be released. If the car is being towed with the front wheels on the pavement, the ignition switch should be unlocked to release the steering wheel, with the steering wheel held securely by a steering wheel clamp. The clamp is an auxiliary piece of towing equipment. Another reason for unlocking the ignition switch is to prevent damage to that switch, which could result if it is kept locked.

If sling or wheel-lift equipment is being used, the tow truck operator should attach safety chains to catch the car if it breaks away from the sling or wheel lift. Safety chains should be installed so they don't swing and hit lights, bumpers, or the body.

Once the car is attached to the towing vehicle and you're ready to roll, ride in the tow truck with the operator, who should not exceed a speed of 50 mph.

When you reach your destination, repeat the walk-around inspection to see if the vehicle has sustained damage. If it has, stipulate in writing what the damage is and have the operator sign the document.

How to Start an Engine with a Discharged Battery

Most cars with dead batteries can be jump-started by connecting jumper cables to a live battery in another car. Those cars having manual transmissions can often be started with a push (see below).

Jump-starting

1. With the two cars close together, but not touching, engage the parking brakes and turn off the ignition switches and accessories.

2. If one or both batteries have vent caps, remove them. Wait 30 seconds for battery gas (hydrogen) to escape. Then, cover vent holes with a clean rag.

3. Inspect batteries to determine which posts or side terminals are positive and which are negative. Posts and terminals are usually marked (−) or NEG for negative and (+) or POS for positive. If marks are not visible, the negative post or terminal is the one holding the cable that extends and attaches to the engine. The cable attached to the positive post or terminal extends to the starter motor.

4. Connect one end of the colored (positive) jumper cable to the positive post or terminal of each battery.

5. Connect one end of the black (negative) jumper cable to the negative post or terminal of the booster battery.

6. Connect the other end of the black (negative) jumper cable to a clean metal surface in the engine compartment as far from the discharged battery as possible, such as the AC generator bracket or an unpainted engine bolt. Making this connection may cause sparks, but being away from the battery prevents sparks from igniting hydrogen that the battery may still be giving off.

7. Start the engine in the second (helper) car. Then, start the engine in the car with the run-down battery. If there is no response from the engine, turn off the ignition, disconnect the black (negative) jumper cable from the car with the dead battery, and check to see that the other booster cables are secure. Reconnect the disconnected cable and try again.

8. When the engine starts, let it run at a fast idle for 30 seconds before disconnecting the jumper cables in this order: (a) black (negative) cable from your car; (b) black (negative) cable from the booster battery; (c) colored (positive) cable from your car; (d) colored (positive) cable from the booster battery.

Push-starting

Before you attempt to push-start a car with power steering and brakes, consider the fact that as long as the engine isn't running, power steering and brakes aren't working. It takes extra strength to handle both functions as the car is being pushed. Therefore, it's a good idea to run a test by steering and braking the car as it's being pushed at a low speed. If at this point you don't believe you can steer and brake effectively, forget the push-start method and use jumper cables and a booster battery to try getting started.

Line up the bumpers of the two cars. Place the manual transmission in the car with the dead battery into second gear, depress the clutch, and turn on the ignition switch. Wave a hand to signal the driver in the other car to begin pushing.

When the speedometer shows a little more than 10 mph, let out the clutch and press the accelerator pedal a bit. The engine should start as the car accelerates away from the other vehicle.

Finding a Competent Mechanic

The odds of finding a competent mechanic are greater today than ever before. The reason for this lies with a "safety net" for consumers called the National Institute for Automotive Service Excellence (NIASE or ASE for short). The organization was established in the 1970s to organize and promote high standards of automotive service.

The ASE tests mechanics under the auspices of the American College Testing Program. To qualify to be tested, a mechanic must have at least two years of hands-on experience. Tests are given in such skills as repairing and servicing the engine, automatic transmission, manual transmission, differential, front end, brakes, electrical systems, and heating and air-conditioning systems.

Mechanics can take tests in as many categories as they wish and, if they pass, are certified as competent. A mechanic who passes at least one test receives a gear-shaped patch to wear on the shoulder of his or her uniform. Underneath this patch are bar-shaped patches indicating the areas in which the mechanic has been certified.

A good way to look for a competent mechanic, therefore, is to scan the walls of a repair facility for the ASE certification, which is issued when at least one mechanic working for the facility has passed an ASE test. Then, request that a mechanic be assigned to work on your car who has been certified in the particular system that needs to be serviced.

There are these other questions to ask yourself in judging the competency of a repair facility:

1. Is the quality of work backed by a written guarantee for at least 30 days?

2. Does the person you deal with listen attentively to you as you describe the problem you're having with the car?

3. Are there any complaints filed against the facility with the local chapter of the Better Business Bureau?

Index